OUR FLAG STAYS RED

OUR FLAG STAYS RED

by

PHIL PIRATIN

With a Foreword by
William Gallacher, M.P.
and a new Preface by the author

Lawrence and Wishart
London

First published 1948
by Thames Publications

This new edition with a new
Preface by the author 1978
Reprinted 1980

© Lawrence and Wishart
39 Museum Street
London WC1

Printed and bound in Great Britain at
The Camelot Press Ltd, Southampton

Contents

Preface to the 1978 edition   vii

Foreword   xiii

1. "... But No One Asked Me To Join"   1
2. "Our Borough"   10
3. Masses Against Mosley   15
4. Tenants Fight Back   33
5. "Spirit Enough for Two"   50
6. Tea at the Savoy   68
7. "As Ye Sow...."   79

Epilogue   88

Preface to the 1978 edition

I welcome the reprint of *Our Flag Stays Red*, following inquiries and requests from a growing number of people in recent years. I wrote this book in May 1948—actually I did not "write" it; I dictated it to my hard-working and dedicated secretary, Hilda Forbes, who now lives in her home county of North Yorkshire.

The book is in no way a biography; nor is it meant to be a record of my political work in the years 1934 to 1948. In the latter part of that period I held the posts in the Communist Party of – among others – London Organiser and West Middlesex Organiser. From July 1945 I was Communist MP representing Mile End, Stepney.

The book does not cover any of my experiences in these areas of activity. It is focused on the activity, struggles and achievements of the Communist Party, mainly in Stepney, in which I directly or indirectly participated from 1934 to the early part of the 1939–45 War.

The book was not my idea. At that time, Willie Gallacher and I comprised the Parliamentary Group of the Communist Party, both of us working "a hundred hour week" in and out of Parliament. So I was not looking for some book-writing to do in my spare time.

The book came to be written as a result of discussions in the Communist Party Executive and Political Committees, of which I was a member. We noted the changes taking place in the political situation and the mood of the workers, which was also reflected in the ranks of the Communist Party.

In July 1945 the Labour Party had won an overwhelming majority at the General Election. Before the election the Tories held 358 seats and Labour 164. After the election the Labour Party held 393 seats and the Tories 198. The Services vote was overwhelmingly for Labour. The Labour majority was elected on its programme, "Let us Face the Future", which contained progressive policies, much of which the Communist Party supported. On the first day of Parliament in August 1945, with a newly appointed Labour Government on the Front Bench, a Miner Member of Parliament rose and began to sing "The Red Flag"; all the Labour Party MPs, the three ILPers and Willie Gallacher and I rose and joined in, to the consternation of Churchill and the Tories around him.

This was the situation and mood in 1945. A euphoria permeated the Labour Movement and even affected members of the Communist Party: this new Labour Government, elected after a bitter war against fascism, could now introduce a progressive policy for the people of Britain. However, under the leadership of Attlee, Bevin and Morrison, the aims and aspirations expressed in Labour's policy statement evaporated and, with it, disillusion set in.

The leadership of the Communist Party did not suffer from any illusions in 1945 about the difficulties ahead in ensuring the carrying out of a progressive policy; nor did we have illusions about the enthusiasm of the right-wing Labour leaders for such policies. The Communist Party leadership continued to give guidance and to organise campaigns on the issues of the day, and to keep the aim of socialism before the people and the organised Labour Movement.

In 1948 a fresh campaign was launched around the policies of the Communist Party, involving the Party organisations conducting their activities on the mass issues in a vigorous and militant style. New directives and propaganda material were issued. The object was to restore the class-conscious, fighting tradition of the Labour Movement, and deepen political understanding in the course of the activity.

In this connection Emile Burns, then head of the Communist Party's Propaganda Department, proposed that I should write a book about some of my experiences in creating a mass movement which resulted in the strong support for the Communist Party in Stepney, as shown by the subsequent electoral results. At that time, in early 1948, the Communist Party in Stepney had an MP, two County Councillors—Ted Bramley and Jack Gaster—and twelve Borough Councillors. Emile's proposition was approved, and so my book.

The book and the Foreword, written by Willie Gallacher, are reprinted exactly as published in the 1948 edition. Some footnotes have been added, and the previous "Author's Note" has been replaced by this new Preface.

Soon after the book was published in 1948 I was told by the publishers that it was selling well, and from letters I received I knew that it was popular reading. I even received a letter from a Communist branch secretary in New York, where the book had also been published, telling me how their situation and problems were so similar to ours and how our experiences had helped them.

Several years ago a leading member of the Young Communist League told me that he had read extracts of the book at classes of the YCL, and some of the comrades told him that they found it very "exciting" and wanted to buy the book, which of course was out of print.

The book has also received some publicity over the years around the anti-fascist struggles of the 1930s which mainly appear in Chapter 3, "Masses against Fascism". Nearly twenty years ago Arnold Wesker used this chapter as the basis of the first act of his play *Chicken Soup with Barley*.

About eight years ago BBC 2, and later BBC 1, presented a series of twelve television documentaries, "Yesterday's Witness", one of which they called "The Battle of Cable Street". This too was based on the same chapter in my book, and brought to life very vigorously the struggle against fascism in the 1930s of which that particular event on 4 October 1936 was an outstanding episode and a turning-point.

I was very pleased when I was recently contacted by the organisers of the Cockpit Theatre, London, concerning a play they produced called "Marches", which was particularly being used in connection with the education of senior school children, and which was based, likewise, on the 1930s struggle against fascism, with particular references to the events mentioned in this chapter.

I was also interested to see that in the Socialist Workers' Party journal, *International Socialism* (January 1977), there was an article "Fascism: the Lessons of Cable Street", even though some of its interpretations and conclusions on the anti-fascist struggles were distorted in order to bring them into line with the outlook of that party.

In recent years, with the advent of the National Front racial activities and the urge by all convinced democrats and socialists to persuade the people of the menace of this fascist-orientated organisation, growing numbers of activists have become interested in the struggle against fascism in the 1930s.

Several historical works have been published about the period between the two world wars, such as *Britain in the Thirties* by Noreen Branson and Margot Heinemann, which present a broad study of the period. *Our Flag* does not pretend to qualify to rank as such a history.

It is a true story of Communist life and activity, in one area of London, in moving masses of working people into action for their just demands and for the causes they supported or learned to support. It tries to show the Communist Party branches and groups as living organisations, with constant problems and differences of views, but above all united, under strong leadership, to win great numbers of working men, women and young people to organise, struggle and—though not always—to achieve.

While I am not required to draw the book's lessons for today's political activists, there is one issue I wish to refer to—the inflammatory issue of racism and the National Front activities. Some organisations on the left appear to be trying to identify the current struggle against racism with the anti-fascist struggle of the 1930s. This is a mistake, and to pursue this line can result in setbacks for the democratic movement.

Fascism in the 1930s was a movement which developed in every advanced capitalist country as a counter force against the growing socialist and Communist Parties. It began to grow soon after the First World War, as an extreme section of those hostile to the then young socialist Soviet Union, when "the spectre of Communism" really began to "haunt Europe". Under whatever name or guise, it was a political movement to maintain the capitalist system by destroying the Communist and socialist parties and the Trade Union movements. To win support it used nationalist demagogy and with it racist discrimination.

By the mid thirties, there were fascist regimes in Germany, Italy, Portugal and Austria, a fascist State Governor in the USA (Huey Long), and the fascist-led military attack on the democratic Spanish Government. Further, the fascist governments of Germany and Italy had shown they were motivated for war against their neighbours or for colonial power (Italy and Abyssinia). The struggle against the fascists in Great Britain was therefore part of a world-wide struggle against fascism and war.

In Britain, the struggle was to stem the advance of fascism at the same time as directing our main attacks against the Tory Government which, on the one hand, was responsible for the appalling economic and social conditions which the fascists used to launch their nationalistic propaganda and, on the other—in all kinds of ways—attacked the democratic rights of the people and gave tacit, and sometimes overt, support to the fascists (both in Britain and overseas).

The failure of the capitalist and democratic governments to stem indigenous fascism, and the aggressiveness of the German, Italian and Spanish fascists, resulted in the 1939–45 War.

It is clear from this very brief summary that the present struggle against racism is different in all major respects from the anti-fascist struggles of the 1930s. With the advance of Socialism since 1945 in many countries and the liberation of most of the former imperial colonies, I doubt whether we could see a world-wide reactionary development such as we then experienced.

In Britain the Labour Movement is now stronger and more confident in its ability to fight back reaction. Nevertheless, backward economic and social conditions remain. Our main aim must be to rally masses of people for a struggle which will eliminate the festering social and economic conditions in which fascism can thrive, and in the course of it rouse a movement of people in action that will begin to understand that fascism, in all its various forms, is incompatible with social advance and must be destroyed.

Our exposure of racism should lead to constructive action. We should actively support organisations and committees which defend the interests and rights of Black and Coloured people, and be prepared whenever necessary to fight alongside them against racist provocations or attacks. At the same time, we should call for the strengthening and the more vigorous implementation of the present Race Relations Act outlawing racism, as well as endeavour in every way to win for this struggle the active participation of the many decent, democratically-minded people in the Labour and progressive movement. Thus, once again as in the thirties, it must be the masses who oppose the racists and fascists.

As the first edition of this book was published thirty years ago, describing events which went back fourteen years before, I have wondered what kind of book I would write today about that period. I suppose I would write a different type of book, owing to the passing of thirty years and the national and international events we have experienced and suffered in that period.

Would it therefore be a better book? No. Because the essence of the book written in 1948 was to express the zest and spirit of those who took part in the struggles of the previous decade, and to recapture these qualities in the disappointing and confusing atmosphere created by the Labour Government of the time. I think that *Our Flag* made a useful contribution to the wider forms of propaganda at the time in raising the level and quality of our campaigning.

I particularly hope that many young people in the Labour Movement will read this book; there is much in it that relates to the current situation. Those who pass through the ultra-left organisations, for whatever reason they join them, need to know about the history of the Communist Party. There are many more local histories to be written up. Each main centre has its history of struggle which young people should learn about, so that they can derive strength from the spirited struggles of an earlier generation.

In recent years, in the Communist Party and in the Labour Movement, there have been many sharp discussions and disagreements. In the period described in the book there were also different views on various matters. But the keynote of the events I described was mass activity; so the different views which people had were mostly directed onto the mass problems and the role and activity of the Communist Party concerning them. This was healthy and beneficial. I sometimes used a home-made cliché: "Argue but act; debate but do!" At our branch and group discussions there was not much tolerance for those who "argued" without "acting".

In rereading the 1948 edition to prepare my notes for this Preface I have reflected on events which brought back to me memories of our struggles and achievements. I have also stopped to ponder over past mistakes. Above all I have remembered many comrades, only some of whom are mentioned in the book, who were involved in the activity and struggles of that period. Not only those who have remained staunch to the cause of our Party, but others who have left our ranks as the political vicissitudes of the past thirty years have had their effect. When they, like I, look back on their lives, they too will recall with a sense of personal pride those years of intense activity, enjoyment in achievement, and the encouraging support of thousands of working men and women seeking and responding to the leadership of our Party.

Phil Piratin
April 1978

Foreword

DURING the 1945 election campaign we had great hopes that Harry Pollitt would be returned for Rhondda East. But in the last days of the campaign the terrific anti-Tory feeling expressed itself in a sort of tidal wave for Labour which, to our bitter disappointment, engulfed our hopes for Rhondda and kept Harry out of the House of Commons. But then unexpected news came from Stepney. Unexpected to the Party comrades and the people generally throughout the country, but not unexpected to the comrades in Stepney—Phil Piratin had defeated the sitting Labour candidate and carried the Mile End division of Stepney for the Communist Party. This was something to talk about. How was it done? What sort of lad was this new Communist Member of Parliament? These questions were being asked wherever I went. For, believe me, it is not easy for a Communist to win a seat anywhere with all the cards, as they are, stacked against him. It is not necessary for the Labour candidates to have anything to recommend them. They do not have to work out or explain any policy. A few demagogic phrases is all that is required and the machine does the rest. I look around me often in the House and I say to myself, " I wonder how in God's name any selection conference, presumably of workers' representatives, came to select such a specimen as a Labour representative." So many do not differ in the slightest degree from the Tories, and the last thing on earth they would think of would be to associate themselves or their families with the working class. But once selected, the votes are almost sure. That is why so many Liberals, despairing of parliamentary preferment, have now found comfortable seats in the Lords and Commons through the Labour Party.

But here was some one entirely different. Phil Piratin, who had not been lifted into Parliament by the machine, but who had fought the machine and defeated it. Here he was, a lad courageous, intelligent, with a fine grasp of national and international affairs, and with a very high measure of political judgment to guide him in his work in the House of Commons. The "machine" men could only stare at him and wonder how he had succeeded in doing it. But not only had Phil got into Parliament, but in the local elections in Stepney the Communist Party candidates were returned in ever increasing numbers.

Is it any wonder questions were being asked? Now all these questions are answered in *Our Flag Stays Red* in the clear and attractive manner that typifies Phil's speeches in the House of Commons. *Our Flag Stays Red* is the story of a long-drawn-out fight. Not just a story of an individual or a Party group, but a fight of the Stepney people. A fight against appalling housing, a fight for health and happiness against rack-renting landlords and against the complacency and opportunism that was eating its way into the vitals of the Labour Council.

Read here how a start was made in a notorious rack-rented block of houses known as Fieldgate Mansions, and how it developed into the fierce battle of Langdale Street Buildings and Brady Street Mansions. In these latter cases the fight against the landlords went on for five months. The landlords had refused to negotiate. They issued eviction orders to some of the most active tenants. Thus, as Phil says: "The battle now began in earnest. Barbed wire barricades were placed around the entire blocks. Pickets were on duty day and night. Only those who lived in the buildings or could give reason for entering, or who were known tradesmen, were allowed to enter." Of course, the police took action, quite brutal action, in support of the bailiffs. You can read in these pages what the tenants were up against. Nevertheless the fight was carried forward to a successful conclusion, thanks to the courage and endurance of the Stepney people and the wise, unfaltering leadership of the Communist Party in the area.

I hope every Party member, every worker who reads this book, and all of them should read it, will give special attention to this part. The lesson is of first importance. We may work like supermen to better conditions in a given area. We may have a considerable measure of success so far as actual improvements are concerned, but if we do not succeed in getting the people themselves to participate in the fight to achieve such improvements, our success will only be of a partial and passing character. For it is only when the people take part in the fight that they get the opportunity to find out for themselves who are their false friends and their real champions, and what are the politics behind the conditions against which they are are battling. It is only through their activity that they are able to test out the correctness of Communist policy, try out their own strength, and learn the lesson of unity. It is only in the midst of such activity that the Communist Party has the opportunity to explain its policy as a whole, and so assist the people in their struggle towards power.

These lessons are of particular importance today when partial struggles are developing around a whole host of economic, social, and political questions. As I write, the result of the Gorbals by-election has just come through. With Peter Kerrigan we had a candidate of whom any member of the Party could feel proud. He had a great team of comrades working for him, including Harry McShane, who has a record of service that is unsurpassed. Much of that service has been given in the Gorbals. Gorbals, like Stepney before the blitz, is a crowded area with housing conditions that are a disgrace to any civilised community. In the circumstances of the by-election we did well, exceptionally well. In face of the barrage of Labour, Tory, Liberal press and radio lies and slanders, against all the forces, religious and secular, that could be mustered by the unholy alliance of dollar Socialists and dollar Tories, we polled over 4,000 votes. It was a real blow to our opponents. They never dreamed that we could muster such support, in view of the vicious campaign of prejudice that had been aroused against us. All credit to the comrades in the Gorbals for the great work they have done, the loyal service they have given.

But it is not enough. They must bring the Gorbals people into the fight. Not yet have they succeeded in doing so, except on one or two rare occasions. The Gorbals people have been waiting on Labour doing something for them for forty-two years. Now it is necessary to get the Gorbals people to stop waiting, and to start in real earnest doing things for themselves. Gorbals can be won for the Communist Party; of that I am sure. But it means work, work directed towards activising the Gorbals people. " The Gorbals Story " is a sordid enough affair. It is not the true story of the Gorbals. That has yet got to be written. The Communist Party started the first chapter in the by-election. The Stepney story may help us to write the rest.

But in Stepney there was not only the fight against slum landlords, there was the truly heroic struggle against Mosley and his fascist thugs. Having, however, succeeded in bringing the people into active participation in the fight against the landlords, it made it easier than it otherwise would have been to bring them on to the streets in their tens of thousands to block the streets and to issue their challenge, " Mosley and his thugs shall not pass ". Not all the police of London could intimidate them or break their ranks. It is a real inspiration to read this part of the book and to realise the strength of the people once they are aroused to action.

All this activity was going on while Labour councillors and Labour leaders were skulking behind empty, meaningless phrases, used as a cover for their own weakness and capitulation. Our comrades in Stepney gave good leadership to the people against the slum landlords and against the fascist thugs. They gave good leadership in the fight against Chamberlain—the fight for peace. When war did break upon us, the people of Stepney felt it in all its destructive horror: whole streets wiped out in the blitz, people crowded into insanitary shelters. Our comrades carried on through it all, fighting for proper shelter conditions, for the use of the Tubes, and for the supply of bunks so that the people might get the possibility of sleep. I remember going down on one occasion to visit the shelters in Stepney. I was met by Phil Piratin. It was my first acquaintance with him. I was amazed, as we went from one shelter to another, at his coolness and poise. I was never at ease when an air-raid was on. Always I felt a bit queer. Of course, I could hide my feelings, maybe others did the same, but I kept thinking, " This lad is hardened to it, he'll face anything." So it seemed to be with a group of comrades in Stepney. Day and night they were on the job, under conditions that will never be forgotten by the people of Stepney. As a result of my visit to Stepney and to other areas, I wrote out a report on shelters which I submitted to the Home Secretary, who was then Sir John Anderson. Later on he informed the House that I had brought before them the question of sanitation and sleeping accommodation. Still later, when Morrison was Home Secretary, the work started in Stepney had made such progress that bunks were ready and sanitation provided for. It was all in hand and well ahead before Morrison got the job, but he took all, or most, of the credit for these improvements. But our comrades in Stepney were the pioneers. Don't take my word for it. Read *Our Flag Stays Red*, the facts are here.

WILLIAM GALLACHER, M.P.

1

" . . . . But No One Asked Me To Join "

MY EARLY life had no associations with the working-class movement. Not that my family was remote from the class struggle. On the contrary, I have heard my father tell how, when I was born (15 May 1907), at the tail end of a large family, he had no money to pay for the midwife's expenses. He had to pawn many of his books—he was a great reader and scholar—in order to pay for the expense of bringing me into the world. But my father was religious, and the difficulties and hardships were not put down to the fault of society but to " God's will ".

I was born at 2 Coke Street, Stepney. At the age of about two we moved around the corner to 13 Greenfield Street, and here I remember my early childhood. Neither of these places exists now, they were both destroyed by enemy action in 1940. I grew up as other Stepney children did. We played in the streets—and played " rough ". I remember battles between Greenfield Street and Settles Street boys with sticks and stones. There was no grass. The nearest tree was at Whitechapel Church. It was an outing to go to Victoria Park. Sometimes there would be trouble between Jewish boys and Gentiles.

When I was about four, the " Siege of Sidney Street " took place. This was the occasion when "Peter the Painter" and his accomplices were trapped in a house at Sidney Street, Stepney (about half a mile from my home), and when Churchill, then Home Secretary, called out the Guards. I tried to reach the place but was hustled back home by an adult neighbour. When my father was told where I had been found he clouted me, but I didn't mind.

I remember crying when I was about the same age, but not for being clouted. One day I set off with another boy, about half a year my junior, collecting tram-tickets. This was a favourite pastime with East London children in those years. Since then, of course, children have had cigarette pictures. During the First World War I remember that the habit of children was to collect shrapnel in the streets the night after an enemy air-raid. It was remarkable indeed the things we collected as "shrapnel". Screws, nails, nuts, bolts, every piece of metal which had fallen off some passing van, was to us "shrapnel", and as such, a war trophy taken from the enemy.

At four, however, I was collecting tram-tickets, and off I went with this other boy after dinner one day. We walked for miles. For those who know the district, we walked past Stratford and far into Leytonstone. It was getting dark when we decided to turn back. We reached home at half-past eleven, tired, hungry, but happy. We had between us thousands of tram-tickets, stuffed into every pocket. My friend lived three doors away. I said "goodnight" to him and knocked at my door. I was welcomed with a first a clout, and then—"Where have you been?" I explained where I had been, and then received a good hiding, which I knew had to come. I was then told to go to bed. I did so, and took with me my tram-tickets. Suddenly there was a banging at the door. My friend's father had come to inquire of my father what he was going to do about my misleading his boy (I was four, he was three and a half!) My father, to show his sense of paternal responsibility, called me down and asked me for the tram-tickets. These I gave him, and he put them into the fire. At that, I cried.

These things happened to most East London children. We took the beatings for granted. Many of our parents had no time to "understand us". They worked hard from morning till night, and very rarely had time to spend with the children.

The Second World War is still so fresh in my mind that I find it very hard to recall scenes of the First World War. I remember when the first zeppelin was brought down at Potters Bar. From Stepney, about fourteen miles away, we could see it coming down in flames, and we cheered. I remember when the Armistice Day was announced on 11 November 1918. There was no school. I was then eleven years old and I and a gang of boys went to the West End "to see the fun".

"...BUT NO ONE ASKED ME TO JOIN"

It was about this time that I began to question our "way of life". As I have mentioned before, my mode of life at home was based on religion. My father undoubtedly was very sincere in his belief, and with it a very upright and respected man. I had reached the age, however, when I no longer accepted "God's will" as the answer to awkward questions. And looking back now, I must have asked many awkward questions. I followed my father's belief and religion, and as much as a boy can be sincere, I was sincere in my faith, and in carrying out the various precepts. I remember being shaken, however, when on one occasion I asked my father's friend, Dayan Rabbi Chakin (a "Dayan" is a Jewish judge), how it was possible for the Chief Rabbi of Germany to call on the Jewish people to fight in the Kaiser's armies, and the Chief Rabbi of the United Kingdom to call on the British Jews to fight in the British armies, both Chief Rabbis knowing quite well that their fellow Jews would be fighting each other. I was quoted all kinds of references, the essence of which was that the Jewish people are strangers in a strange land, should be grateful for their shelter, and should conform with the decisions and policy of the reigning Government. This, of course, didn't satisfy me, as it was in conflict with the teachings of religion, in which I then believed, regarding international brotherhood. It was abhorrent to me to think of one Jew fighting another. In later years I met Christians who told me that they had similar thoughts at the same time.

I believe it was these conflicting thoughts on the First World War that set me on the path of thinking more seriously about life around me, and in particular, about the merits of my religious faith. Nevertheless, when I was at school—about thirteen years old—we had a "Mock Parliament". There was a small group of Socialists. Most vocal was a lad named Harris, and he certainly could "rant", but I and my particular set of friends at school looked upon him and others as "freaks". In later years I have looked back and wondered how I could have been so remote from the Labour movement, then developing rapidly in East London, as to think such things. I have been told of the existence of Socialist Sunday Schools in those years, after the First World War, but somehow I never knew of them at the time. I also knew nothing of the Communist Party which had formed a branch in Stepney during this period.

I wanted to be an architect. The headmaster, who considered me a " bright kid ", thought it a good idea. So did my father, but he pointed out that it was economically impossible. My older brother and sisters didn't take any interest. My mother had died when I was thirteen. She had been ill for many years, and I hardly remember her. After several months' argument I left school and went to work to learn the fur trade. That job did not last long because the firm closed down. I then went to other trades, but I was unhappy, and at about seventeen I left home. I did all kinds of jobs, including a period at sea. Later I settled down in business, got married, and led a normal life.

About this time I was thinking seriously on many questions. When I left school I continued to read a great deal, particularly scientific and philosophical works. I remember in those days being very impressed by Bertrand Russell. He had a lucid mind. I even bought some of his books, which I still have. (This is a sad reflection on Bertrand Russell, for many worth-while books are no longer on my shelves, having been " borrowed ", while Russell remains.) Later, Shaw wrote his book, *The Intelligent Woman's Guide to Socialism and Capitalism*. I read it and thought that it answered everything. I discovered later that it did not, but it stimulated me to read other books. I was a regular borrower from the Whitechapel Library. There was no one to guide me. Over a period of several years I read social and political works covering a very wide field. The first book I attempted to read by Lenin was *Empirio-Criticism*. I remember reading a chapter and then wondering what I had read—I didn't understand a word of it.

About that time I went to a series of lectures at the Bethnal Green Library given by T. A. Jackson. He was very impressive; so impressive that a number of questions which I had to ask him were never uttered, as I was afraid of being " annihilated ". But he explained many things which I could not understand in my readings.

At this time I became involved more and more in political discussions. The General Strike had been and gone. The 1931 Crisis was looming ahead. In Stepney, more and more conversation turned

"...BUT NO ONE ASKED ME TO JOIN"

to politics. But I did not take part in any activity. Had some one asked me, I might, but no one did and I didn't think of it either.

In 1932 I saw activity. The "Hunger Marchers" were in London. One contingent was stationed in Stepney, and I helped with supplies. I was very keen in my support. I would have joined the Communist Party had some one asked me. Some of my best friends were Communists, but no one asked me to join. I didn't join.

Later I was active in the "Anti-War Movement". I cannot remember how I got drawn into it. I might as well have got drawn into the Communist Party, but no one asked me.

About 1934 some of my friends in the Communist Party—in particular, I remember "Shimmy" Silver and Lew Mitchell—asked me to join the Communist Party, but by that time I was such a close supporter of the Communist Party, that I didn't see the need for joining it! I eventually joined that year, a few days after the Mosley Rally at Olympia on 7 June.

This was to be his greatest rally. The fascists had already staged meetings in the main provincial centres, and earlier in the year had held a meeting in the Albert Hall. Twenty thousand fascist supporters were expected at Olympia. Many of these were transported by the B.U.F. from various parts of London and from the provinces. No less than three thousand of the Fascist Defence Force (the tough core of the B.U.F.) were brought to Olympia on this occasion.

The Communist Party went into action, but before I describe some of the events, I think it is necessary to understand the political situation and developments at that period.

The nation was slowly emerging from the worst economic crisis in living memory—three million unemployed, severe under-nourishment, many middle-class people, professionals and small tradesmen, affected, in some cases bankrupt. The traditional political parties had no solution. The Labour Government of 1931 could have taken drastic measures, but the leaders had been sold to capitalism. The National Government placed the burden of the crisis on the working people, which in turn intensified the crisis.

Abroad fascism was dominant in Germany. The disunity of the working class, and in particular the hatred of the right-wing Social Democrats for the Communists, which prevented any possible co-operation, gave the Nazis the opportunity they wanted. In February that year the fascists took power in Austria. In the same month the fascists attempted a coup in France, but the Communist Party, at the head of the working class, was too vigilant and the coup failed.

The fascists in Britain, in such circumstances, had made some headway, supported by many capitalists and industrialists and by the Rothermere Press. Fascists thugs and hooligans were treated benignly in British courts. Openly supported by numbers of Conservative Members of Parliament and Peers, they sought to duplicate the example of the fascists in Germany and Austria.

The Olympia meeting on 7 June 1934 was to be the zenith of a series of rallies throughout the country. Thousands of influential people had been invited; no tickets were on sale, but could only be obtained direct from the B.U.F. and were not available to anybody without some handle. Mosley was out to impress the "people who mattered". He aimed to display the strength and discipline of his organisation, the kind that would "stand no nonsense" from the working class. He wanted to impress others who "comprised the backbone of England" with the same sentiments as those expressed at the time by Sir Thomas Moore, M.P. for Ayr Burghs, who wrote in the *Daily Mail*, 25 April 1934:

> "What is there in a black shirt that gives apparent dignity and intelligence to its wearer? . . . There was little . . . if any, of the policy which could not be accepted by the most loyal followers of our present Conservative leaders. . . . Surely there cannot be any fundamental differences of outlook between Blackshirts and their parents, the Conservatives? For let us make no mistake about the parentage. . . . It (the B.U.F.) is largely derived from the Conservative Party. . . . Surely the relationship can be made closer and more friendly."

Now, if only all Conservatives and other "respectable" citizens would think that way, then Mosley was "a dead cert" for dictator, should some critical political situation develop.

How to expose Mosley and the fascists for what they were? How to bring home to the British people the nature of this beast? The Communist Party rallied thousands of workers to go to Olympia. Previously, some hundreds of Communists and other anti-fascists had been able to obtain tickets for the meeting. The thousands who rallied outside, however, could obtain no access to the meeting, the way being barred by a thousand police. Inside the meeting hundreds of courageous anti-fascists, men and women, exposed Mosley, though they were battered and mauled by the Blackshirt thugs for the slightest interruption or protest.

I was one of the thousands outside the hall charged again and again by the police, mounted and foot. We stood our ground and watched the anti-fascists ejected from the building, many in a state of collapse, bleeding profusely, clothes torn and tattered. From outside we only heard stories of what was going on inside, and could use our imagination when we saw the victims. Mosley's thugs could only get away with this brutality because of their protection by the police who stood by, cynical and indifferent, as the beaten-up victims were thrown out of the building. Any suggestion made to the police that they should prevent this barbarism was at its best met with a " mind your own business ". In one mounted police attack when, by pushing their horses sideways, the police were able to pen a number of us against the wall, some one shouted to one of the senior mounted police that his duty would be better served in preventing the dastardly actions taking place inside the Olympia. I heard this senior officer shout back: " Get back to your slums, you Communist bastards."

Some of the comments made by impartial observers not only gave an impression of the scene inside, but showed at the same time that the anti-fascists, by their own sacrifices, had won the day in exposing Mosley. Mr. Geoffrey Lloyd, Tory M.P. for Ladywood Division of Birmingham, and Parliamentary Private Secretary to Mr. Baldwin, stated:

> " I am bound to say that I was appalled by the brutal conduct of the fascists. . . . There seems little doubt that some of the later victims of the Blackshirt stewards were Conservatives and endeavouring to make a protest at the unnecessary violence of the proceedings. . . . I can only say it was a deeply shocking scene for an Englishman to see in London. . . . I could not help shuddering at the thought of this vile bitterness, copied from foreign lands, being brought into the centre of London. I came to the conclusion that Mosley was a political maniac, and that all decent English people must combine to kill this movement." *Yorkshire Post*, 9 June 1934.

The Very Reverend Dick Sheppard, who went to the meeting on the invitation of Mosley's mother and was not concerned to comment on any of the brutal ejections which took place in the Hall, said:

> " I confine myself to one of the instances I witnessed when I got into a corridor leading to the exit. A young man who had been ejected was showing signs of the way in which he had been handled. I was horrified at the monstrously cruel treatment to which he was now subjected by the fascists in charge of him. He was bleeding on the face and was gasping for breath. He

was being chased down the corridor by a horde of Blackshirts. Some collared him by the legs, others by the arms, and held in this way, he was beaten on the head by any fascist who could get near him. There was a large crowd of them." *Daily Telegraph,* 11 June 1934.

Workers at Olympia testified to the National Council for Civil Liberties as to the preparations that were made by the Blackshirts prior to the meeting.

The events of that night have been dimmed by the subsequent record of fascism during the Second World War, but the exposure organised by the Communist Party was an eye-opener to millions in the country, and a political lesson of great importance to many thousands. People like myself (I was there with two other friends who held very much my own views) understood as clearly as daylight the truth of Lenin's thesis in his *State and Revolution.* Only the deliberately blind could claim the impartiality of the police, and of the courts, on that and the following days.

Yet, on 9 June, only two days after Olympia, the *Daily Herald* published a letter from Mr. T. R. West, then Labour M.P. for North Hammersmith:

"The Communists, by smashing Blackshirt meetings, are as usual, aiding the fascists, and gaining public sympathy for them. We of the Labour Party do not fear the effect of Mosley's speeches. In any event, let them be heard, for free speech is still precious today, although the Communists are such opponents of it."

There was plenty to learn that night for people like myself, and plenty to do; not all the police " got away with it ", and we waited until the meeting was ended, and the fascists began to leave. Some of them paid well for what they had done that night. Mosley later tried to prove that more fascists were taken into hospital than anti-fascists. This is quite possibly true. The anti-fascists had organised their own first-aid posts in different places near the Olympia, where hundreds were attended to by anti-fascist doctors. The reason? Police persecution and victimisation. The police had a pleasant habit of gathering lists of anti-fascists who found their way into hospital as a result of fascist savagery and later on things began to happen. A policeman would call and tell the wife some hair-raising story about her husband's nefarious doings. Employers were informed by the police and anti-fascists found themselves sacked. Sometimes these lists had a way of getting into the hands of the B.U.F. who then put the names on to their " threatening list ". This is why the anti-fascists had their own first-aid centres.

"...BUT NO ONE ASKED ME TO JOIN"

That night I was proud of the anti-fascists, the working class, and particularly the Communist Party. I could have kicked myself for not being a member of a Party whose lead I was so proud to follow. That night, going back to Stepney, I told " Shimmy " Silver, then a group leader of the Communist Party, that I wanted to join. The next week I attended my first meeting.

2

"Our Borough"

WE HAVE all learnt a lot since 1934, yet so much has had to be learnt the "hard way". It is true that when you have learnt something by experience it is well learned, but the world would never have moved forward if each one had to learn from his own experience. Perhaps we ought to spend more time in the exchange of experiences, pay more attention to others. I wonder whether my experiences when I joined the Communist Party in 1934 are still repeated.

The group was active. We sold the *Daily Worker* and we held meetings. A meeting was held at least once a week at Vallance Road. Later on, when traffic lights were placed at the corner, we held our meetings at Fulbourne Street, a hundred yards farther along Whitechapel Road. The main speaker that we had was Lew Mitchell—a very confident open-air speaker. Very rarely did we have the use of an amplifier, and one of the first qualities of an out-door speaker was the power of his voice—a very useful factor, even today, but fortunately not so important as it used to be.

When I discovered that we carried out no activity around Blackwall Buildings (sixty-year-old tenements), I raised the question, but was never given a satisfactory explanation. It seemed to some of us that the group, though active in a propaganda sense (in addition to meetings and *Daily Worker* sales we had some of the most enthusiastic whitewashers), was not associated with the workers, and certainly was failing from the defects inherent in the British Socialist movement so well described by Lenin in *Left-wing Communism*. The only mass work which was carried out was that amongst the unemployed. Silver, the leader of the group, was at the same time a leading member of the National Unemployed Workers' Movement. In fact, in July he had to relinquish group leadership in order to concentrate more on the work he was doing among the unemployed. Though this question of " going to the people " was raised on a number of occasions, the matter never went much further at that particular period. Yet there were so many things to " go to the people " about.

Stepney was almost an entire slum. The borough had gone through a long period of decline, and a complete overhaul was called for. Stepney could, and should be, a great centre of a great city. In 1939 the population stood at about 200,000—nearly as many as in Leicester or Plymouth, but herded into an area only a fraction of their size.

Just east of the City of London, Stepney itself, as a village, goes back a thousand years in the records. William the Conqueror built the Tower of London outside the City of London itself, within the present boundary of Stepney.

At the beginning of the sixteenth century Erasmus wrote to the Vicar of St. Dunstan's, Stepney, Dean Collett: " I come to drink your fresh air, to drink yet deeper of your rural peace." About the same time, Sir Thomas More wrote of Stepney: " Wheresoever you look, the earth yieldeth you a pleasant prospect."

Then came the expansion of British commerce and industry. Stepney, adjacent to the City of London, and bordering on the river Thames, developed into one of the most important sections of the Port of London.

In addition to the port and the roads which led into it, industry developed. More and more people came to live in Stepney. Country folk who came to work in the city found a home in Stepney. Irish labourers who came to work in the docks lived in the dockside areas of Shadwell. The spread of population developed eastwards from the city. And the contrast is to be seen in the early nineteenth century in Dickens's own descriptions of different parts of Stepney. Readers will remember his description of the Spitalfields area in *Oliver Twist*, the hang-out of the rogues and thieves. Some of these slums are still there. At the same time, in *Nicholas Nickleby* he describes the country cottages at Limehouse, only a mile or so from Spitalfields. A few years later, with the extension of the London port, and the opening of the West India Dock, the Limehouse country cottages made way for industrial dwellings.

From the very first expansion of Stepney's population the housing and the surroundings were completely unplanned, and were of the poorest type and quality. The houses were crammed into the streets, and the people into the houses. By 1870 there were 275,000 people in a borough of two and a half square miles, and by 1900 there were 300,000. The population was very mixed; not only was there the usual population to be found in ports and dock areas, but many foreigners coming into this country settled in Stepney. They included Germans and French. The French Huguenots, persecuted in the seventeenth and eighteenth centuries, fled to England and a large community settled in Stepney. One of the largest of Stepney's synagogues was formerly the site of the Spitalfields Huguenot Church. The Spitalfields silk-weaving trade was developed by the French.

In conditions such as these it is understandable that Stepney achieved some notoriety. Even when I was a child one heard of streets where police would not even walk in twos, let alone singly.

Towards the end of the last century, and until the outbreak of the First World War, large numbers of Jews, escaping from Tsarist tyranny and from the reactionary rule in other countries such as Austria, Hungary, and Rumania, came to England and many of them settled in Stepney. By this time, however, the population began to move further afield, particularly into Essex, and others to North London. Yet the housing situation did not improve, for while the people moved out, industry and trade moved in. This was particularly so on the western side of the borough near the city.

At the turn of the century the population began to decline fairly rapidly at the rate of about 2,500 a year, so that in the thirties the population was reckoned at about 200,000. Understandably, many of those who left the borough were the younger and less conservative-minded people. In the thirties in particular there was a double attraction to leave Stepney Borough—better housing and more opportunities for work.

New industries were opening up in other parts of London, better equipped and in many cases more amenable. At the same time, industry began to leave Stepney. This was particularly so in the case of clothing and furniture, which were becoming more rationalised. In 1934 every industry in Stepney, even the breweries, was suffering from the crisis. There were over 11,000 unemployed. There was widespread discontent and bitterness. Life in Stepney was grim, though Stepney folk had their own Cockney gaiety, and with a few bob in their pockets found their own means of escaping the grimness and drabness around them. But without a few bob. . . .

So when I joined the Party there were plenty of " mass issues " of which each Party member could tell his own tale. Outstanding were the demands for work or adequate unemployment benefit, and for homes. The unemployed were active, led by the National Unemployed Workers' Movement which looked after the individual unemployed at the same time as they fought for improved conditions collectively. At work problems were arising in which Communists were playing an active part and strengthening trade-union organisation. Particularly was this so in the clothing industry. But the Communists were not giving an adequate lead to the people of Stepney in obtaining better homes, schools, playgrounds, health facilities, etc.

What was the position with other political parties? The Conservative Party had a majority on the Stepney Council (this they had regained in 1931, having lost it in 1922), and in Mile End, one of Stepney's three Parliamentary Divisions, there was a Conservative M.P. (This seat had also been re-won in 1931 from Labour.) These positions were won again by Labour in 1934 and 1935 respectively, thus ending an unhappy interlude and a very significant one for Labour. As one who was born and bred in Stepney, I could not understand how a Conservative could get a majority in any part, except on the grounds of disgust with Labour and in the absence of any other alternative party.

The Liberal Party, so far as Stepney was concerned, was expiring. The Liberal Party had had a tradition in Stepney, and particularly in Whitechapel and St. George's Division, where their main support came from the tradesmen's section and from a large proportion of the Jewish community. Barnett Janner held the seat in Whitechapel and St. George's, which he won in 1931 from Labour and which he was to lose to them in 1935. Some time after he lost his seat in Whitechapel and St. George's Barnett Janner, having in mind, no doubt, that the British public required his services in Parliament, joined the Labour Party. He now represents West Leicester on the Labour ticket. He was not the first to do this, for he followed Lord Nathan who, as Major Nathan, represented Whitechapel and St. George's on the Liberal ticket; in 1924 he lost his seat to Labour, and he, too, joined the Labour Party in 1934.

The Labour Party itself was both strong and weak. Strong in the support it had from many of Stepney's workers, in the potential support it could have had from the trade-union organisations. Weak in its complacency and opportunism, which began to set in as power grew. As for Socialism—I recall a conversation with a prominent Labour Party member in Stepney at a Mayoral reception in 1937. I had asked him whether we weren't " all Socialists ". He replied: "No! I am Labour. You might find about four or five Socialists out of the sixty-nine Labour on the Borough Council."

The year 1934 was therefore a period in Stepney, as in many other parts of the country, where not only were the working class suffering in their conditions, and through unemployment, but they were likewise suffering the pangs of disillusionment with Labour. At the same time they were now feeling the Tory "crack of the whip" which they had invited by ousting Labour in 1931. When one realised these things, one felt "if only there were a mass, powerful Communist Party to show the workers the real way forward, and to offer them an alternative Government." As I look back in writing on that period, so much wiser now than then, I ask myself what alternative will the workers see when disillusionment sets in once again, as it is sure to do in view of the present Government's policy.

The Stepney Communist Party was enthusiastic and hard-working on issues that were clear, such as anti-fascism and unemployment. Complex issues, or those calling for balanced presentation, were often over-simplified, and sometimes avoided. Activity was undertaken almost solely by directive of higher organisations of the Party, rarely from local initiative, and hardly ever as arising from the needs of the people. The Stepney Party did not yet have its roots in the people. It had not yet "won its spurs"—in the coming years it was to do so.

3

Masses Against Mosley

THE FASCIST movement, led by Mosley, had been growing since 1932, during a period of severe crisis and unemployment, supported by many of the capitalists in their fear of the advance of the working class. The British Union of Fascists had been able to hold meetings and carry on their propaganda in all parts of the country. Everywhere, led by the Communist Party, the working class opposed the fascists. The authorities gave full support to the fascists, and were blatantly partial in every respect. Mosley himself was in contact both with Mussolini and with Hitler, and was receiving funds at least from the former.

About this time a change began to take place in the activity and propaganda of the B.U.F. More emphasis was laid on the anti-Jewish character of their propaganda, and activity was concentrated in areas where Jewish people lived. Until this period—1935—the fascists did not particularly emphasise the anti-Semitic part of their propaganda.

They began to change the direction of their propaganda as the circumstances in Britain themselves changed. The deep crisis had passed and Britain's industry was gradually recovering. The grounds of middle-class discontent and ruling-class fear were therefore beginning to recede.

At the same time the General Election of 1935 gave the Conservatives, led by Baldwin, a very large majority, unexpected by them and by the Labour Party. In view of the Conservative Party's reactionary policy during the years 1931-35, it was anticipated that there would be once again a swing to Labour, at least with the degree of support manifested in 1929. But whereas then Labour won 288 seats, in 1935 Labour won only 148. The reason for this was not because of confidence in the Tories. On the contrary, Baldwin announced a year later that his party during the election campaign had subscribed to the League of Nations Union peace campaign, though it was not their policy, only in order to get the votes of the millions who supported that policy. The main reason for Labour's defeat was that during these years it had disrupted the fight against the Tories and the so-called " National " Government. For the unemployed, it not only did nothing, but obstructed the efforts of the Communists and the National Unemployed Workers' Movement. It did its utmost to weaken the fight against fascism in Britain, which the working class was conducting, led by the Communists. It had left the fight against war to the Communists and the anti-war movement, content to tail along behind the Tory policy of appeasement. The opportunity of developing a mass working-class movement of class solidarity with the German workers, oppressed by Hitler, had been ignored by the Labour and trade-union leaders. Membership of the Labour Party was at its lowest for many a year. Hence the victory of the Conservatives in the 1935 election.

But in these new circumstances the fascists had to find new scope for their activities, and particularly a basis on which to attract support. Thus began the violent anti-Semitic campaign, modelled on the Nazi technique, and most notably felt in areas of London and the larger provincial towns where Jewish people congregated. East London was the centre of Mosley's activity. Branches were opened up at Bethnal Green, Shoreditch, Hackney, and elsewhere. Full-time organisers, well-provided premises, all these were paid for. The appeal was made to the worst elements, and the basest sentiments. Jews were " taking away your jobs ". Because of the Jews " you had no home ". The Jews were the bosses and the landlords. The capitalist Jew exploited you—the Communist Jew was out to take away your liberties, your freedom, and your private property ! It didn't make sense, but put over with flourish and showmanship it was propaganda calculated to gull the more backward sections of the community. The B.U.F. won recruits, particularly from the younger elements in Shoreditch, Bethnal Green, and Stepney. Jews were attacked every time when they were outnumbered or in no position to defend themselves, such as elderly people or children. Strife and tension characterised the atmosphere in East London in those years.

What to do about this menace? The Conservative, Liberal, and Labour Parties " deplored ", but said that the authorities should be able to deal with any actions which transgressed the law (at least in those days they " deplored "—today they no longer even " deplore "): but the authorities, namely the police, did not deal with the fascists. On the contrary, they were deployed by the score and the hundred to protect them from the growing opposition of both Jew and Gentile alike. As this opposition developed, the Labour Party shrieked to their members, directly and through the *Daily Herald,* to keep away and not be misled by the Communists. That is exactly how the Labour Party's prototype, the Social Democratic Party of Germany, behaved before Hitler came to power. Many Labour members and supporters did not heed this advice.

Only the Communist Party stood out as the forthright opponent of fascism, and of the National Government which supported and protected it. No one in East London and particularly Stepney, in those days, was unaware of this fact. A number of Labour members acknowledged this leadership of the Communist Party and regretted the weakness of their own leadership. Such " premature " anti-fascists were condemned, and in some cases expelled, by the Labour Party.

During the recent war every one was " anti-fascist "—even Chamberlain. Now it is no longer fashionable. Under the plea of " free speech " the Labour Home Secretary, supported by Tories and Liberals, allows Mosley to re-establish his fascist movement.

While the Communists were clear-cut in their opposition to fascism, the problem of how to present this opposition became more and more vexed. To expose the fascists, to rouse the workers to refuse to give them a hearing: to carry out our own propaganda, to expose the National Government as the main enemy of the people which was deliberately inflicting the fascists upon them—these activities built up the anti-fascist movement. But were they enough?

I remember well the constant discussions in the Stepney branch committee of the Communist Party. There were those who said:

"Bash the fascists whenever you see them." Others among us asked ourselves: How was Mosley able to recruit Stepney workers? This, in spite of our propaganda exposing the fascists. If they saw in the fascists the answer to their problems, why? What were the problems? Did we, in our propaganda, offer a solution? Was propaganda itself sufficient? Was there more that ought to be done?

One evening Mosley held a meeting at Salmon Lane, Limehouse, Stepney. In order to settle this problem in my own mind I went along to this meeting, made myself inconspicuous, and watched to see the support which Mosley had. When the meeting ended there was to be a march to Victoria Park Square, Bethnal Green, another of Mosley's strongholds. I was curious to see who and what kind of people would march. The fascist band moved off, and behind them about fifty thugs in blackshirt uniform. Then came the people. About 1,500 men, women (some with babies in arms), and youngsters marched behind Mosley's banner. I knew some of these people, some of the men wore trade-union badges. This had a terrific effect on my attitude to the problem, and I went back to the Stepney branch committee determined to fight this. The case which a minority of us put up in Stepney was that while we would fight Mosley's thugs, where did you get by fighting the people? We should ask ourselves: "Why are these ordinary working-class folk (it was too easy to call them *lumpen*) supporting Mosley?" Obviously because Mosley's appeal struck a chord. There were certain latent anti-Semitic prejudices, it is true, but above all these people, like most in East London, were living miserable, squalid lives. Their homes were slums, many were unemployed. Those at work were often in low-paid jobs. Therefore we urged that the Communist Party should help the people to improve their conditions of life, in the course of which we could show them who was really responsible for their conditions, and get them organised to fight against their real exploiters. This conception was not accepted by the majority of the branch committee in Stepney, and it had to be fought for for months. Branch meetings were verbal battlefields, but we won in the end. And because we won, this book can be written. In the next chapter I will describe how we cut the ground from under the fascists' feet—the basic, solid, slogging work of exposing fascism to its own supporters. In this chapter I deal with the physical battle against the fascists.

The epic of this fight was 4 October 1936. The fascists were claiming membership running into thousands in each of the London boroughs. As many as 4,000 were claimed in Shoreditch alone. Earlier in the year the fascists had held a march through the northern part of East London. Now they announced their intention of marching from Royal Mint Street (near the Tower Bridge, the most western part of Stepney), along to Aldgate, down Commercial Road, to Salmon Lane, Limehouse, where a meeting was to be held, and then on to Victoria Park Square, Bethnal Green, where there was to be another meeting. When the date of the fascist march was announced the London District Committee of the Communist Party gave immediate consideration to the development of anti-fascist action and was concerned as to whether a Youth Rally already announced for 4 October in Trafalgar Square could continue to be held. Representatives of the District Committee discussed the problem with the Stepney branch leaders. Meanwhile, however, the propaganda against the fascists had "caught on" in East London. So fierce was this that a deputation of the five East London mayors went to see the Home Secretary, Sir John Simon (now Lord Simon), to ask him to ban this march. He refused. The " Jewish People's Council against Fascism and anti-Semitism " which had been carrying on a vigorous campaign against fascism and anti-Semitism, in contrast to the passive, supine attitude of the Jewish Board of Deputies (the accredited authority for the Jewish community in the country), now organised an East-London-wide petition. A hundred thousand signatures were obtained in the course of a few days, calling on the Home Secretary to forbid this demonstration. He refused. East London was in a ferment. The Stepney Communists sensed this. At a joint meeting with officials of the London District Committee it was decided to ask the youth to call off their meeting in Trafalgar Square and to devote the full resources of all Communist organisations to the anti-fascist action against Mosley. Once this decision was reached, the most powerful campaign of propaganda and preparation took place, unequalled in any other action of recent working class history with the exception of the 1926 General Strike.

The slogan was issued: "The fascists shall not pass." This had more than a local meaning. This slogan was inspiring the Madrilenos at the same time in the defence of Madrid against the fascists. Steps were taken to bar to the fascists all roads leading through Stepney. The first thing was to rouse the workers to take part in this great action. The second was to decide what the nature of the action should be, and the third was the direction of large numbers of Londoners along the lines of the decisions we had taken.

Scores of meetings were held in all parts of London, but particularly East London, in the days before that memorable Sunday. Thousands of posters, hundreds of thousands of leaflets, and hundreds of gallons of whitewash were employed in advertising the counter-demonstration. Approaches were made to trades councils, trade unions, and Labour Parties to participate. Many did, in spite of the counter-propaganda put over by almost every other section of the movement. The Labour Party, the *Daily Herald*, the *News Chronicle*, the Jewish Board of Deputies, all appealed to the people to stay away. Everything was done to damp down the working-class anger. Communists were condemned as "trouble-makers", but in spite of all this slanderous misrepresentation the appeal of the Communist Party was responded to by thousands of Labour Party members and supporters. On that occasion the leadership of the Communist Party was undisputed.

The days preceding 4 October were used by the fascists to work up a terrorist atmosphere in East London. Windows were smashed, old men beaten up. These things they did by way of intimidation, but they were nothing to what they did after 4 October by way of revenge. These actions could not intimidate the working class. The Communist Party propaganda was effective and successful.

What should be the character of the action against Mosley? It was felt that the workers would rally in large numbers, and plans were made accordingly. With the fascists gathered at Royal Mint Street they could march up Leman Street, past Gardner's Corner, along Commercial Road. This was their advertised march. Where else could they march if they were to make their way through Stepney, which was their main objective, reach the eastern part of Stepney, and so on to Bethnal Green? They could travel eastwards, either along The Highway or along Cable Street. The Highway would in itself be a defeat for the fascists, as it was right down by the dockside, and off the main stream of traffic and population. It would certainly be interpreted as "going in by the back door". Cable Street was a possibility, but the police, we knew, would be apprehensive because it was a narrow street with many side streets and alleys, and it also had a reputation of being a somewhat "rough" district. It was decided, therefore, to rally the workers firstly in a block at Royal Mint Street, so that the fascists would have to fight to get into The Highway, but we reckoned that Number One braggart, Mosley, would resist any police direction along The Highway at all.

In view of the attitude of the Home Secretary and of the police, we estimated that the main efforts would be to carry out the route as advertised. We therefore made the main call to rally to Gardner's Corner, Aldgate. We reckoned that if the fascists should attempt to pass through Cable Street, we could handle them in a different way. We would build barricades. For the Cable Street defence we called particularly on the local dockers and other inhabitants; they rallied to a man.

It was necessary to ensure strict discipline, as we knew of the existence of many *agents-provocateurs*, and we also anticipated that all kinds of bluffs would be pulled. There was constant communication between responsible Communists "at the front" and headquarters. Motor-cyclists and cyclists were organised, and were indispensable in ensuring contact. First-aid depots in the care of anti-fascist doctors and nurses were opened up in a number of shops and houses near the scenes of battle. Meanwhile, we had taken steps to ensure that should, by any chance, the fascists get through, they would not be able to hold their meetings. We had comrades standing by their platforms at Salmon Lane, Limehouse, and at Victoria Park Square, from seven in the morning. I shall never forget the look of dismay on the face of "Shorty" (6 ft. $4\frac{1}{2}$ in.) Brookes, when, as secretary of Bethnal Green Communist Party, he was instructed that he, his comrades, and supporters must hold the platform at Victoria Park Square for the Communist Party, and not allow the fascists to take over. All day long they stayed there until the evening, when we held our "Victory" meeting.

We also ensured that should the fascists make some détour through the City and north through Shoreditch and Bethnal Green, we should be informed of any such move. We therefore organised a number of suitable persons to act as observers, who were constantly on the telephone to headquarters, informing us about fascist movements. Over a hundred phone calls came through in two hours from these "observers".

On the morning of 4 October there was a feeling of impending battle. Loudspeaker vans, organised by the Communist Party and the Jewish ex-Servicemen's movement, were touring all the morning. The Young Communist League band, led by Harry Gross (later killed in Spain), marched round the streets with slogan-banners. The mood of the police was already to be seen early in the day. The Jewish ex-Servicemen's Association, composed solely of members of the British Legion, had organised a morning march around Stepney to advertise the counter-demonstration. They wore their medals and decorations. Led by the British Legion standard, they conducted their march in excellent discipline, and were very well received. At about half-past eleven they were about to pass westwards along the Whitechapel Road crossing New Road. The police had put a cordon across this and refused to let them march. New Road is about half a mile from Gardner's Corner, therefore it was evident that the police intention was to interfere with this peaceful demonstration by the ex-Servicemen. A fight took place with the police for the rights of the ex-Servicemen to march in their own borough. Mounted police attacked. The British Legion standard was fought for; eventually the police captured it, and in front of the eyes of these ex-Servicemen, tore the British Legion Union Jack to shreds and smashed the pole to pieces. The police had begun to "maintain law and order".

From an early hour people began to gather at Aldgate with the police shoving them around. Then the police really moved in. Six thousand foot police and the whole of the mounted division were on duty, posted between Tower Hill and Whitechapel. Sir Philip Game, the Commissioner of Police, had his headquarters in a side-street off Tower Hill. Police wireless vans moved around, reporting frequently. A police "observation" aeroplane flew low overhead. Every chief police officer in the Metropolis was on duty. Special constables had been drafted in to take the place of the "regulars" withdrawn from other parts of London.

After the police came the fascists. They came in coaches from all parts of London and the country. Here and there were scuffles, coach windows were smashed and some early casualties taken away. The fascists were due to march at 2 p.m. The police, aiming to keep Leman Street clear, tried to hew a path through the crowd, estimated at at least 50,000, that blocked the whole of Gardner's Corner. At the junction of Commercial Road and Leman Street a tram had been left standing by its anti-fascist driver. Before very long this was joined by others. Powerless before such an effective road-block, the police turned their attention elsewhere. Time and again they charged the crowd; the windows of neighbouring shops went in as people were pushed through them. But the police could make no impression on this immense human barricade.

It was obvious that the fascists and the police would now turn their attention to Cable Street. We were ready. The moment this became apparent the signal was given to put up the barricades. We had prepared three spots. The first was near a yard where there was all kinds of timber and other oddments, and also an old lorry. An arrangement had been made with the owner that this old lorry could be used as a barricade. Instructions had been given about this, but when some one shouted "Get the lorry!" evidently not explaining that it was in the nearby yard, some of the lads, looking up the street, saw a stationary lorry about 200 yards away. They went along, brought it back, and pushed it over on its side before any one even discovered that it was not the lorry meant to be used. Still it was a lorry, and supplemented by bits of old furniture, mattresses, and every kind of thing you expect to find in box-rooms, it was a barricade which the police did not find it easy to penetrate. As they charged they were met with milk bottles, stones, and marbles. Some of the housewives began to drop milk bottles from the roof tops. A number of police surrendered. This had never happened before, so the lads didn't know what to do, but they took away their batons, and one took a helmet for his son as a souvenir.

Cable Street was a great scene. I have referred to "the lads". Never was there such unity of all sections of the working class as was seen on the barricades at Cable Street. People whose lives were poles apart, though living within a few hundred yards of each other; bearded Orthodox Jews and rough-and-ready Irish Catholic dockers —these were the workers that the fascists were trying to stir up against each other. The struggle, led by the Communist Party, against the fascists had brought them together against their common enemies, and their lackeys.

Meanwhile, charges and counter-charges were taking place along " the front " from Tower Hill to Gardner's Corner. Many arrests were made, many were injured. It was the police, however, who were carrying on the battle, while the fascists lurked in the background, protected by a " fence " of police. Mosley was late. As soon as he arrived, in a motor-car, a brick went clean through the window.

It was later rumoured that Sir Philip Game had been on the telephone to the Home Secretary, and had pleaded with Sir John Simon to forbid the march. Sir John was adamant. Sir Philip Game, however, made up his own mind. He forbade the march and told Mosley to argue it out with Sir John Simon. The fascists lined up, saluted their leader, and marched through the deserted City to the Embankment, where they dispersed. The working class had won the day.

Immediately thousands of leaflets were issued by Communists, calling for a victory demonstration at Victoria Park Square, where Mosley was to have held his rally. The workers lined up and, led by the Y.C.L. band and headed by a number of injured workers with their heads bandaged and bloody, off they marched to Victoria Park Square. That night dozens of meetings were held in all parts of Stepney and East London to teach the lessons of that great day of victory. Some meetings went on until midnight. There had never been so many meetings held simultaneously. We'd never had the speakers. Suddenly the speakers were there. Those who were tongue-tied the day before were full of expression that evening; they had a message to give; they were proud and they were confident. They no longer needed to be told " have confidence ". The crowds were jubilant. The police were absent.

The effects of 4 October were many, not only in Stepney, nor in the country, but from all parts of the world we later heard the repercussions. I recall a letter from the British lads then fighting in Spain, later to be formed into the British Battalion of the International Brigade. For them it was the greatest inspiration that their friends and comrades in London were fighting the same fight with the same enthusiasm as themselves.

That week the Edinburgh Labour Party Conference was taking place. The question of Spain was the outstanding item on the agenda. Bevin urged non-intervention. Those who opposed him were strengthened many times by the fighting spirit of London's workers. It was as much " news " at Edinburgh as it was in the streets of London.

As for the repercussions in Stepney, I find it impossible to describe the reactions of the Stepney people. In Stepney nothing had changed physically. The poor houses, the mean streets, the ill-conditioned workshops were the same, but the people were changed. Their heads seemed to be held higher, and their shoulders were squarer—and the stories they told! Each one was a " hero "— many of them were. In the barber shops there was only one topic of conversation for the next fortnight. Even the racing lads slipped up on placing their bets in time for the races while in keen conversation as to the part they played on that Sunday. People from the docks and the factories would take their workmates who had not been in Stepney on the Sunday to show them the scenes, and where they had played their part.

The " terror " had lost its meaning. The people now knew that fascism could be defeated if they organised themselves to do so. There was towards the Communist Party who had organised the people a warmth of feeling that the lies of our enemies will never eradicate.

The hundreds of injured, and the 150 who were charged in Court, many of them receiving harsh sentences from the magistrates, did not detract from the victory. On the contrary, many of those who were victims of the battle joined the Communist Party and carried on the struggle.

The Communist Party had shown itself capable of leading the working class in keeping the fascists off the Stepney streets when the Government and the police, ignoring the requests of the London citizens, had attempted to foist the fascists upon them. New heights of working-class discipline were being achieved. On the following Sunday, 11 October, the London District Committee of the Communist Party organised an anti-fascist demonstration through East London, through the heart of the "blackshirt" area in Bethnal Green. This demonstration was meant to be not only a "victory" procession, but to inspire with confidence the working class of the area through which we passed; to strengthen them in their struggle against the fascists in their midst. We expected provocations, and strict instructions were given for the firmest discipline. Capable marshals were appointed, no one was to leave the ranks, no matter on what provocation, whether physical or verbal. The test for the marshals was more difficult than for the marchers. The marshals were picked for toughness, but were told that in no circumstances were they to be tough. They were abused, spat upon, had filth thrown on them, but there wasn't one case of a Communist marshal breaking discipline. That demonstration was a huge success. It ended up in Victoria Park with a great meeting, and undoubtedly must have had a demoralising effect upon the fascists and their supporters in the parts of East London through which it marched.

The fascists began to lose ground, resorting to acts of terror and provocation. The police did nothing. A little girl of seven was thrown through a plate-glass window in Mile End Road. She was cut and lost one eye. No one was arrested. In Stepney there were very few who were not aware of the role the police were playing in protecting the fascists who were attempting to terrorise the district. The numbers of certain police who seemed to delight in attacking the workers were noted and announced at public meetings. If they happened to be present, they would be pointed at and described, so that there would be no misunderstanding. They were then informed in no uncertain terms that the people of Stepney did not want them there. In most cases they disappeared to another division.

The people of Stepney learnt that if "law and order" were to be maintained they would have to do it themselves, for the police were acting as their enemies. We kept law and order.

The Communist Party offices were the centre. Any incident of fascist provocation was immediately notified, and a call would go out to the people to rally. We took the shortest cuts. On one occasion, for instance, when some fascists were reported in Whitechapel, not far from the Rivoli Cinema, Barney Becow (now of the Wembley branch), who had a very "fog-hornish" type of voice, bought a ticket, went into the cinema near the front, and then shouted: "Communist Party calls all out; fascists in Whitechapel." He and almost the entire audience then left the cinema. Old folk, a few women, and children were left behind. The fascists were soon bundled out of Whitechapel and the people went back to the cinema to watch the rest of the performance.

The discussions on the Stepney Communist Party branch committee as to the best way of combating the fascists had now gone stages further. Some of us said that we had to win the supporters of the fascists away from them, if not completely to us; that we could only do this by working amongst them, by carrying on our propaganda and dealing with their problems. When this view was at one time put forward by myself, the then secretary of the branch said sardonically: " It's all right for you to talk, you are not working in that area." I was then working in the St. George's North-West area, whilst the main centre of the fascists' activity was the Mile End Centre area. The leading comrade there was Bert Teller. I immediately offered to switch over with Bert. This offer was difficult to reject. The deal was done. At first it was not easy to convince the comrades in Mile End Centre of the need to change their mode of work. The clash of opinion in the Party had also created some personal animosities. I found myself still arguing what should be done rather than doing it. So I took a short cut.

I went to a meeting of my former group, and asked if two comrades could be allotted to work with me. This was agreed, and I asked for two who I knew were in complete support of the kind of work I was advocating, and who were absolutely dependable in every way. One was Sid Greenberg, now a leading member of the Wembley branch, the other was "Chirps" Steinberg, recent victor in a Stepney Council by-election. We began to canvass in Duckett Street, Ocean Street, and other fascist strongholds. The going was hard, and there were some difficulties. We were concerned primarily with getting organised action of the people on tenants' problems and such issues.

At the same time, knowing that many of the young fascist supporters indulged in physical training at the Ocean Street L.C.C. Institute, arrangements were made for a number of good lads from the Blakesley L.C.C. Physical Training Institute, almost every one of whom was a good anti-fascist, to transfer to Ocean Street, in order to mingle with the fascists, sport with them, and at the same time to put over our propaganda. I cannot help laughing now in recalling the directions that were given to these lads. They were all good physical specimens, and at the same time had some fair political understanding. I was rather worried about a gleam in some of their eyes, and they were warned that there was to be no "politics" when they were having a couple of rounds on the mat with the fascists. These lads did excellent work in neutralising and winning over these young fascists. On one occasion, in the course of a spar, one of our lads knocked a fascist unconscious. When he was called to account for this, he was apologetic, but explained that it was due to this other man hitting too hard for a friendly spar, and so he had lost his temper and given him one for the count. This particular lad later won every boxing match that he ever contested in the R.A.F.

From all this, our propaganda, our canvassing, our talks, something began to stir. And in June 1937 the turn was made. Often, almost always, you can point to a certain event which indicates a decisive turn in a situation. This is what happened on 6 June 1937.

There is a block of buildings in Mile End Centre called Paragon Mansions. In Stepney we also have a "Paradise Row", a "Fleur-de-Lys Street", a "Flower and Dean Street", and a number of others with similarly mellifluous names. With such names you could always expect the worst—and you were rarely wrong. Paragon Mansions should have been condemned by the local authority forty years before, but it was still there. People were living there, raising families, and landlords were taking the most exorbitant rents possible for these slums. We had been canvassing and selling the *Daily Worker*. A committee of the tenants had been formed, which won the sympathy and support of some public-spirited local citizens. An expert survey of this dilapidated block of buildings had been drawn up by a group of progressive architects and technicians headed by Michael Shapiro.

One day we were told that two of the families were to be evicted the next day. In one family there were five children, and in the other six. I was immediately called to the scene. I was curious to know why these people themselves had done nothing in the matter, and why they had not referred the matter to the Tenants' Committee. I discovered that in both cases they were members of the B.U.F. and obviously wanted no truck with us. One family would have nothing to do with us whatsoever that evening. The other was prepared to listen. We pointed out to them, so far as we could judge by the papers and court documents, that the bailiffs calling the next day would have the law on their side, and the only thing to do was to prevent the bailiffs gaining access. This might mean a fight, but we convinced them that it would be well worth while. They agreed. Late as it was—about 11 p.m.—we called a meeting of as many tenants as possible in one of the rooms, put to them our proposals, and they agreed to make the fight. As a result of this solidarity the other family the next morning decided to take part. Meanwhile, in conversation, we asked this member of the B.U.F. about to be evicted what the fascists had done for him. He said that he had raised the matter, but they had no intention of doing anything. This was a very valuable piece of information to be used by us in disillusioning many of the B.U.F. supporters.

Very early the next morning the barricades were being arranged at the entrance to this block of buildings. No one could get up the stairs without removing these barricades, but there were balconies overhead from which any one trying to get access without permission could be bombarded with ease. From a nearby grocer's shop old and mouldy flour was obtained, with the grocer's compliments, and this was placed upstairs at strategic points. The two flats themselves were locked and barred from inside. Some of the women had to be persuaded by the Communists that it was inadvisable to use anything more than the flour and pails of water. Some were disappointed. All was ready for action when the bailiffs were due to arrive.

Looking at it from across the road it was a strange scene. Three weeks earlier there had been the "Coronation" celebrations of King George VI. A children's party had been organised, and the buildings were still be-flagged and pictures of the King and Queen were still hanging. The bailiffs approaching these buildings would have seen poor tenements bedecked with flags and bunting, now somewhat faded. As they approached, however, they would see the barricades and the tenants lined up on the balconies in a militant mood, prepared for action. Some may ponder on this contrast. To us in East London it was no contrast. The national press, and all the propaganda machinery in the country, other than that of the Communists, has in the early months of 1948 carried on a most vulgar, stupid, and hypocritical boosting of the Royal Family; earlier, at the time of the wedding of Princess Elizabeth, and later, on the anniversary of the marriage of the King and Queen. When they toured East London in April the papers said that the crowds came out on to the pavements. Maybe not so many turned out as the papers described, but if the capitalist class and their press lackeys want to delude themselves that this response was an indication of faith in capitalism and subservience to the State, this scene, still fresh in my mind, at Paragon Mansions, Stepney, tells another story.

The bailiff and a colleague came along. When he saw what had happened, he said he would have to call the police. I persuaded him to hold over action while I and a colleague went to the County Court to try and get the Order postponed, to allow of further discussions with the landlord. Unfortunately, the Clerk of the County Court could not see his way to postponing the Order. We were not able to make contact with the landlords. Therefore it meant battle.

When we got back to Paragon Mansions, the bailiff was informed that there was no intention of allowing him entry. He tried to convince the tenants about it, but was unheeded. He went away. It was a very simple calculation as to how long he was to be. Paragon Mansions was about seven minutes' walk from Arbour Square Police Station. Within half an hour the bailiffs were back with forty police. The police were a little dismayed when they saw the kind of job they had to do, and the Inspector gave the order for the barricades to be pulled away. Then out came the flour, and the police were smothered. The water soon followed and when this got mixed up with the flour they were completely *hors de combat*. The police made no headway in removing the barricades, and after a while they were called off and stood at a distance while the police Inspector went away, no doubt for further instructions.

Meanwhile, the morning had flown and lunch-time had arrived. Suddenly some one shouted, " The kids, what about the kids?" and we immediately realised that the children, who had been sent off early in the morning to school and were now coming home for their dinners, couldn't get up to their respective homes. But in a flash the solution was found. In the back was a small courtyard, with a type of balcony running on the first and upper floors. A thick rope and a dustman's wicker basket were obtained and a couple of " strong-arm " men were placed on the balcony and called the " lift-men ". As the children came home, each one was put into this basket and hoisted up. Later on, after their dinner, the " lift " returned the kiddies to ground level. They had a lovely time, and supported the eviction fight wholeheartedly. One of the strong-arm men was Tubby Rosen, and I believe that his participation in that day's action enthused him for the whole of the struggle, as a result of which he later played a tremendous part as secretary of the Stepney Tenants' Defence League. Incidentally, most of us who took part were at work but had not gone in that day. An unsuccessful Communist candidate in the council elections a few months ago told me that on the day of the election he had no help at all until the evening, after working hours. When I asked him why hadn't some of the comrades taken time off for this very important job, he almost apologised for them. So far as I can recall, in Stepney we had little difficulty in getting people to stay away from work in order to take part in some working-class action.

During the lunch hour many workers gathered who were passing to and fro on their way to work, and also from the nearby factories. Charringtons' Brewery is only a hundred yards away, and we obtained a box from the same helpful grocer. I stood on this box and held a meeting explaining the issues involved, the conditions in the buildings, the attitude of the landlord, the law—which operated against the working class, the role of the police, and the purpose of the eviction fight which the Communist Party had organised. There was general support and sympathy. This also had an effect, I believe, on the police attitude, and that of the bailiffs, who saw public opinion mounting against them. When negotiations were later resumed, the police made a half-hearted effort to persuade us to remove the barricades, but eventually the bailiffs agreed not to take further action and to hold the whole matter up for a fortnight. During this time we would be able to negotiate with the landlord, or at least arrange alternative accommodation for the tenants concerned. This was a victory, for we could not expect more in the circumstances.

The news went round very quickly, the barricades came down and the " ammunition " was disposed of. The lessons did not require being pressed home. B.U.F. membership cards were destroyed voluntarily and in disgust. Every one in the buildings seemed to have relatives in the nearby streets, and the news went round much more quickly than the leaflet which the Communist Party distributed to the whole of the neighbourhood, explaining not only what had taken place, but the fascist demagogic attitude and the Communist Party action in the matter. This was the first action substantially to prove the line that we had been fighting on the Stepney branch committee.

The tenants' issues now took on a new form. In the next chapter we deal with them, but this is how they emerged in the fight against fascism, and in the prolonged, and sometimes bitter, controversy on the Communist Party branch committee. We were now supplementing our propaganda with positive action. The kind of people who would never come to our meetings, and had strange ideas about Communists and Jews, learned the facts overnight and learned the real meaning of the class struggle in the actions which now followed.

4

Tenants Fight Back

STEPNEY has been, and is, a happy hunting ground of the slum landlord. Workers in Stepney and other parts of East London pay more rent in relation to the space occupied, conditions and amenities, than middle-class people in suburban homes or modern blocks of flats. The worker gets less relative value for his money, as in the case in almost everything. It is a well-known saying in the clothing trade that the man who buys a good suit or overcoat, for which he may pay three times the price a working man may pay, still has far better relative value, for his suit lasts very much longer, wears better and always looks well-made.

The slum landlord takes advantage of the friendly Conservative councillors or weak-kneed, inefficient Labour councillors. He makes his money primarily on the misery of the tenants and on the *absence* of repairs and decoration. In the " estate " business, when a businessman buys property in which he expects " good-class " tenants, he must keep it in good condition and constantly in repair and well-decorated. Hence he makes his profits because of the quality of housing that he provides.

In the case of the businessman who buys slum property there is no question of attracting the tenant. Because of the housing shortage for the working class, there are always working-class tenants waiting for such accommodation. In many cases the rents were controlled (this, of course, was the pre-war position; now there is rent control on all such working-class houses), and therefore the landlord would often hesitate before charging more than the rent allowed by law. How then was he to get his profit? Obviously by reducing his costs to the very minimum. That meant no repairs or decoration if he could help it. Hence the amount of his profits was in inverse ratio to the amount of the repairs and decoration he provided. In many cases the landlord was known to argue that the places were not worth repair; this was often true, but neither were they worth rent. Many of these places were, and are, so badly deteriorated that the landlord could well have been in fear of getting involved in heavy repair expenditure, or even having the whole property condemned by the local authority, but unfortunately for the tenants this was very rare indeed. In such cases the landlord would aim to get his money back in the shortest possible period, and then dispose of the property for whatever it would then bring. I know of one case where a landlord bought slum property and, apart from paying his agent's fees for collection of rent, incurred no expenditure whatsoever. The annual net amount of the rent he was collecting was 50 per cent of the money he had paid for the whole property. He held on for three years. In these three years, therefore, he got his money back, with an additional 50 per cent on his original capital outlay. He then sold the property for one-half of what he paid, to some other equally notorious slum landlord. His total profit was 100 per cent on his original outlay. This man happens to be quite a pleasant person, a good husband and a good father, and quite charitable. To him it was a business deal. To the people living in these tenements it was hell.

The sanitary inspector was sometimes called in and he would send an Intimation Notice, but no one took any notice of that and the sanitary inspector knew that no one took any notice of it. But that was the routine. The tenants did not know that the next step was a Statutory Notice to the landlord, not informing him but instructing him to do the work. The tenants knew that they had tried, that the sanitary inspector had tried, and that nothing had happened, hence, " What's the use?" Some would say, " Well, we know there is corruption ", and so on, and so on.

The housing problem was, and is, of course, wider than the matter of conditions and rents. Above all, houses with space and amenities were required which would at once solve the overcrowding and put the slum landlord out of business. The Stepney Borough Council had had many years in which to provide such homes, but had put up very few. Nor were private landlords putting up new houses in Stepney. In the years before the war about three or four small blocks of flats had been put up in Stepney at rents from 30s. to 50s. They were not meant for the workers.

At the time I joined the Communist Party in 1934 its activities were mainly those of a propagandist character. In the factories Communists were prominent amongst trade unionists and shop stewards in organising their fellow-workers for better wages and conditions. The same attention, however, was not paid to the conditions in the homes and to the struggles against the landlords.

At the end of September 1934 a new group was formed, of which I was elected leader. I suggested that we ought to be taking up the issues of the people in the locality where we were active, in Fieldgate Street area. There was general agreement. But we were not yet clear how to develop the people's struggles. Each weekend we would canvass. We would do fairly well. We sold the *Daily Worker* and literature. Many of the people were friendly. But there were no "issues". Our canvassers would ask the people, "Have you any problems?" and they would say "No!" But there were problems—what were they? And why did the people say there were no problems, when the places they were living in were so bad? Was it because they were so inured to these conditions? This indeed is one of the most serious features that one discovers in working in the movement. Was it because they were defeatist and felt that it was a waste of time to do anything, and so passed these things off with a shrug of the shoulders?

The main centre of our activities was Fieldgate Mansions—several blocks of some 270 flats. It occurred to me that if the people did not know or wouldn't talk of their problems, we ought to suggest them. But what to suggest? One Sunday morning we were canvassing, and when we had finished I walked around the buildings, looking for something. I walked around, and up and down several flights of stairs, but I couldn't get a hint of a thing. I went home—it was very perplexing. I know that all this sounds almost funny. I have a good laugh over it myself, but this was in 1934, when no one had done anything of this kind in Stepney. Now we know "the score". We know what the problems are, and if some one with Stepney experience goes elsewhere, he knows how to begin on the ground floor. In those days we were feeling our way. There was a difference between helping some one who approached you with a problem (as in the eviction fight), and trying to get people to begin in an elementary fashion to organise to improve their conditions for themselves. We had no members of the Communist Party actually living in those blocks of flats. Later we made members.

That same evening I was restless and felt irritated that somehow we couldn't get beneath this. I decided to walk over to Fieldgate Mansions only a hundred yards away and look around a bit to see if I could get an idea. I walked up a flight of stairs flashing my torch; as I walked down, I saw a flame flickering on a landing and suddenly noticed something which I hadn't done all those weeks previously, nor the same day *during the day-time*—namely, that the stairs were lighted with open gas-jet flares. I knocked at the first door; introducing myself, I asked the woman who opened the door whether or not these things were a danger, and immediately I received a torrent of information, and a cursing of the landlord. *I had found an " issue "!*

I asked the woman whether all the neighbours thought like that about this arrangement. She said, " Yes." I asked: " Can you get some together?" and within ten minutes I was sitting around the table with half-a-dozen women, drinking a cup of tea and listening to their stories about the gas lighting. How the wind blew it out, and the escaping gas could be smelt throughout the whole block. How the children would climb on each other's shoulders and light bits of paper from the flares, and all kinds of other very serious allegations about these conditions. The rest was simple. A letter to the landlord demanding electric lighting; a letter to the electricity undertaking, calling for their assistance. A letter in the press in order that other people in such circumstances should know what was happening in Fieldgate Mansions. This letter brought down the wrath of the gas company, who tried a little intimidation. The letter to the landlord proved quite effective. He had been warned in the letter that if there were any casualties arising from this state of affairs he would be held responsible. We already had one or two instances of casualties we could lay at his door. Within a very short period there was electric lighting on the stairs.

This was the first " issue "—but we made many mistakes. We never organised one full meeting of all the tenants. We never set up a proper representative tenants' committee. We never got the tenants to feel they were doing it for themselves. We never held one public meeting among the tenants to explain the political lessons of the whole campaign—though we did issue a leaflet to this effect. I myself did not involve others in responsibility. I could claim that the whole thing went so smoothly on the lines I have mentioned, that there was no need to do so. But the truth is I never even thought of doing so. Maybe because I was keen to get on with the work now at last we had something concrete to grasp. If that were the case, it was "losing sight of the wood for the trees", for the purpose of our work was not merely to get small improvements in the living conditions of the people, but to lead and organise them so that they themselves should take the initiative.

I did not realise these things then. When I realised them later, I asked myself, was that particular activity valueless? I could answer: "No!" Our propaganda and canvassing went on, and was now much more effective in view of the goodwill extended towards the Party. Further, the tenants in these buildings now began to find issues which were all there previously, but which they hadn't seemed to notice.

There should have been an extension of such activity, both in Fieldgate Mansions on other issues, and in other areas. This, however was not done. Vital national and international issues took the headlines, and called for the consideration of persistent activity by the Communist Party. Italy's rape of Abyssinia, the fascist revolt in Spain, the rise of fascism in Britain. These issues demanded the attention and response of the Communist Party, and detracted from the work that had been begun in organising the people in their homes on their day-to-day issues. While we recognise the principle of "first things first", and the fact that an organisation can only carry out activity according to its forces in number and quality, and while at that period the Communist Party was doing excellent propaganda work in the fight against war and fascism, I feel it was a mistake that this work was neglected.

This mistake was rectified when we really got down to the job of winning Mosley's misguided supporters away from the fascist creed, and in support of Communist policy. We decided to fight on two sectors. On the battle for homes and decent conditions and on the issues confronting the unemployed. We felt that it was on these two grounds that the fascists were making headway. They had established an unemployed organisation at the Labour Exchange, Burdett Road, Limehouse, and were attracting unemployed to their support in the usual corrupt, capitalistic way. Funds were available to make weekly payments to the unemployed who were active in the B.U.F. Facilities were provided for their recreation. Their propaganda was very simple. Jewish employers were responsible for not giving them work; Jewish workers were responsible for taking away their jobs.

We took steps, together with the National Unemployed Workers' Movement, to establish a branch of the N.U.W.M. at the Burdett Road Labour Exchange. There was one in existence at the Settles Street Labour Exchange, but there was no fascist problem here. This N.U.W.M. branch did valiant work in exposing the fascists and in dealing with the individual cases of the unemployed.

In the autumn of 1937 the Stepney Tenants' Defence League was established, with Michael Shapiro as its first secretary, and began to deal with the individual rent and repair problems of hundreds of tenants. Our main point of concentration was the area where the fascists had support, the hardest area. It was later that the work spread to other areas, where such activities were " jam ". As this work developed, and we began to know the problems and how to handle them, a new qualitative change was called for. Instead of dealing with the individual problems within the narrow confines of the landlord-favouring law, it was necessary now for the tenants to organise themselves in a disciplined way and to fight their landlords, even for demands which were beyond their legal rights; for rent reductions, for which there was no *legal* justification; for repairs and decorations which the landlord was not, by law, bound to carry out. We were going to take the fight now into the landlords' camp, to take the offensive.

It was at this time that I came to meet the man who became the leader and organiser of the tenants' struggle throughout the country —Michael Best Shapiro. One evening I was at the Communist Party rooms, discussing some matters, when I was told that a Mr. Shapiro wanted to see me. After a while I left my discussion, aiming to return within a half-minute, and went into the next room to meet Mr. Shapiro. Though he, too, was a Stepney man we had never met each other. Very quiet-spoken, almost diffident in his manner, he explained that he was a lecturer at one of the colleges of the London University; that he was specialising in estate, land, town planning, etc., and was in touch with architects and other such professional workers. They were aware of the tenants' work which was developing Stepney, and would like to help. I don't know whether Michael remembers this discussion, or what he thought of me, but I know that I must have been very curt as I was in the midst of some other discussion which had been arranged previously with a number of other comrades. I listened to Michael and I said: " Yes, I suppose you can be of some use ", and we agreed that he and his colleagues could play a useful part in doing research work and other things of that kind. (One of the first jobs they did get on to in this respect was to prepare the survey to which I referred earlier.)

Michael and I at this first meeting did not go further than that, but before very long the quiet, research-minded Michael Best Shapiro was participating in the organisation of the tenants, leading them, then establishing the National Tenants' Federation with offices in Holborn, London, leading a nation-wide struggle on these issues. In the course of these actions this quiet, modest comrade became a mass leader, working at times at a pace unequalled in my knowledge, with dozens of rent strikes on his hands in different parts of London and the country; travelling around from a meeting of working-class tenants, rent strikers in Stepney or Bethnal Green, on to a meeting of residents in their struggle with a building society in some very respectable suburban area of London; running to catch a train to help the great struggle of the Birmingham tenants in 1939; organising a nation-wide campaign for the revised legislation to prevent the landlords blood-sucking the working class. Michael is now leader of the Communist twelve on the Stepney Borough Council. Yes, he certainly was " of some use ".

The mass organisation of tenants continued. Tenants' Committees were set up in blocks of buildings and streets. The individual issues of the tenants were dealt with by the Tenants' Committee, acting as a kind of shop stewards' committee and dealing direct with the landlord. The tenants were gradually gaining confidence and organisational ability ready for the big struggles ahead.

In August 1938 Bethnal Green joined the struggle. The tenants of Quinn Square, 230 of them went into action. Negotiations had been proceeding with the landlords for rent reductions. These had failed. On 2 August the rent strike began; the collector could not get one tenant to pay rent. This action in Bethnal Green was a direct consequence of the line which we had been carrying out in Stepney. In Bethnal Green the fascists had been more active than in Stepney. Many battles had taken place, but now the Communist Party of Bethnal Green was taking steps to win the workers into class action and away from the fascists. Quinn Square was in the heart of the fascist area. Many of the tenants were members of the B.U.F. The struggle was led by Communists, notably Bob Graves. After two weeks' rent strike they won. All rents were reduced.

At about the same time a rent strike was proceeding in Welwyn Garden City, where 300 tenants were on strike against increased rents imposed by the Council. With these skirmishes taking place, it was the very devil to hold back the Stepney comrades from taking precipitate action. The Stepney branch committee insisted that any action of this kind was not to be in any " red " or " pink " part of Stepney, but where we would strike not only at the landlords but at the fascists, too.

Late in November, Michael Shapiro and Tubby Rosen reported that the ground had been laid in Limehouse. The Southern Grove Dwellings tenants were the first to lead Stepney. Then the floodgates opened. During the December weeks the rent strike at Southern Grove was conducted with solidarity and was watched by the whole of Stepney. It made the headlines in the national press. They won in spite of the landlords pleading bankruptcy, and their alleged inability to make the reductions. The tenants said: " We will take over the whole place and run it ourselves." The tenants got their rent reductions. As soon as this happened, it was followed by rent strikes in Flower and Dean Street, Hogarth Mansions, Brunswick Buildings, Pelham Street, Montague House, Hawkins Estate, Langdale Mansions, Brady Street Mansions, Juniper Street, Commercial Mansions, Lydia Street, Fieldgate Mansions, Duckett Street, Ocean Street, Philchurch Street, Eileen Mansions, Bromehead Square, Fenton Street, Mariner Street, Anthony Street, Settles Street, and Golding Street. What were far more important were the repercussions throughout London and the country at large. The rent-strike idea spread to Clapham, Willesden, Finsbury, Poplar, Bermondsey, Paddington, Battersea, Highgate, Norwood, and Shoreditch. In January 1939 action began among 50,000 Birmingham municipal tenants. Similar actions took place in Sheffield, Huddersfield, Liverpool, Aberdeen, Sunderland, and Oxford.

At the same time a new feature of the struggle was developing with rapid tempo—the fight against the building societies. Here was revealed one of the greatest rackets operating between the wars. The Conservative Governments were not prepared to grant assistance to the local authorities in order that they could build houses for the working class, to be let at reasonable rents. In fact, they deliberately cut down grants for slum clearance, slashed the housing programmes, and consciously encouraged building societies. There was therefore no competition, or very little, with the jerry-builders. What was their racket? Had they built houses to let, within a few years those houses, as the slums which many of them became, would never have been " letable " at the rents which the owners expected to receive in order to make them a profitable proposition. So developed the greatest racket of the time: " Own your own Homes "; " The Briton is an individualist." Wonderful pictures were drawn and millions spent on advertising to show how glorious it was to be the complete master in your own home. Hundreds of thousands, even millions, lapped this up, bought their homes on " the never-never ", £50 down, 17s. 6d. a week. After a few years not only normal decorations but serious repairs were urgently needed for these houses were falling to pieces. The working-class folk who proudly inhabited these homes in the suburbs of London and other cities, and who could only make ends meet by accounting for every penny, found themselves faced with the alternative of dilapidation, or of paying heavy repair costs. Meanwhile the payments to the building society had to continue or else.... I remember the time when working-class rent-payers of Stepney would envy the dwellers in these jerry-built suburban houses, and, of course, many of these people valiantly tried to keep up appearances.

The fight was begun in Kent by Elsie and Jim Borders, who organised the Coney Hall District Residents' Association against the building societies in their area. The Borders themselves took action against the building society in one of the most famous test cases of all legal history. Mrs. Elsie Borders, a working-class housewife, fought the case in Chancery Court against the most learned Counsel. The legal arguments went on for weeks and months. She conducted the case as capably as any top-line, highly paid lawyer. She argued, she examined, she cross-examined; on one occasion she spoke for eight hours in submitting her arguments. Elsie Borders became known as "the modern Portia". While they did not win their case, they exposed the tie-up between the building societies and the builders.

A million jerry-built house-dwellers were agog. They had been "had."; the courts admitted it. But the building societies' friend, the Chamberlain Government, introduced a law to safeguard them. This fight, however, which went on for months, roused suburban dwellers throughout the country. These were not slum dwellers, not labourers—these were people with social "aspirations" and they went into battle under the leadership of Communists like the Borders in all parts of the country, in many suburbs of London, such as Hayes, Feltham, Earlswood, Queensbury, Whitton, and Twickenham, and in scores of other places.

The actions in Stepney gave rise to militancy in other areas where such a feature showed even greater advance in the understanding of the people than in East London. In turn, the spirit of the 50,000 Birmingham municipal tenants, and of the resident owners, gave greater power and morale to the working-class women of Stepney, who in the main conducted these great battles. For battles they were, and all honour to the women. It was they who had to be in the homes when the bailiffs called. It was they who had to take responsibility for picketing every hour of the day.

The actions varied. The tenants were organised and formulated their demands. All kinds of repairs and decorations were specified, and reductions in rents were demanded. The rents varied considerably, particularly between controlled and decontrolled houses. The law defining controlled houses was incomprehensible to the tenants, and the landlords did not hesitate to take advantage of this to defraud them. Irrespective, however, of the law, demands were made for reductions of the decontrolled to the level of the controlled rents, and in some cases demands were made for reductions of the controlled rents themselves in view of the state of disrepair of these places.

In some instances the landlord was " reasonable ". This happened particularly at the later stages when the landlords saw the strength of the tenants, and were prepared to negotiate. Many rent reductions and concessions with regard to repairs were attained without recourse to rent strikes. There is in Stepney a certain slum landlord and housing agent who at that time was the most notorious of all. The Stepney Tenants Defence League was just " rarin' to have a go " at him. They were met with disappointment after disappointment. This particular landlord was shrewder than his associates. He knew when to give in. In Lydia Street, the heart of the fascist area, this landlord, by negotiation, agreed to rent reductions of as much as 12s. 6d. per week. Tubby Rosen wanted a rent strike, but there never was one. It nearly broke poor Tubby's heart!

In some cases, after a week or two, the landlord caved in or negotiated, and a reasonable conclusion was reached. In other cases, however, the fight was bitter. The Brunswick Buildings tenants were out on strike for eleven weeks. Langdale Street Buildings and Brady Street Mansions, both owned by slum landlords, were on strike for five months. These latter battles were particularly fierce. The landlords were firm and brazen. They refused to negotiate and after a while issued eviction orders to some of the most active tenants. The battle now began in earnest. Barbed-wire barricades were placed around the entire blocks. Pickets were on duty day and night. Only those who lived in the buildings, or could give reason for entering, or who were known tradesmen, were allowed to enter.

One day in June the bailiffs, with the police, decided to act. They managed to gain access into Langdale Mansions. The alarm was sounded. The police drew their truncheons. The men and women of the buildings defended themselves with saucepans, rolling-pins, sticks, and shovels. The police were brutal, particularly in their treatment of the women. A cordon was placed round the building. More police, a score of them mounted, were called up. They broke open the doors and forcibly removed the tenants. By the end of the morning the news had spread throughout Stepney. The menfolk left their work to come home. The police would not have attacked as they did, with such " courage ", if they had had the men-folk to deal with. The police, using the dirty tactics not unknown in Stepney, waited until the men had gone to work, and then attacked the women. Some workshops closed down. Thousands of angry Stepney people gathered round Langdale Mansions. The police, sensing the feeling, withdrew. Immediately, the Stepney Tenants' Defence League loudspeaker van toured the area, calling a meeting. Prominent citizens spoke at that meeting, not only in connection with the tenants' fight, but now against the police action. Within a few hours' notice some 10,000 people had gathered. When the meeting ended they marched to the Leman Street Police Station to protest. A deputation of three, including myself, were appointed to go into the police station to make our protest. While we were inside a stone was thrown through the window. At this signal, the police, without a word of command from any officer, immediately drew batons and charged the marchers. It was obviously planned. The throwing of a stone through a police station window by one individual did not call for an attack on several thousands by hundreds of police all prepared for this action. There was some rough scuffling. A number of arrests were made. These actions caused a stir throughout the country. Questions were raised in Parliament. But the Stepney people depended on themselves. Tubby Rosen, on behalf of the Stepney Tenants' Defence League, immediately issued a statement that the 7,500 members of the League would join in a solidarity strike with the Langdale Mansions and Brady Street Mansions tenants, unless their demands were met. The tenants themselves were now filled with indignation, bitterness, and hatred of all who supported the landlords. Messages of sympathy came from many prominent citizens and leaders of the Labour movement. The Communist Party itself lent all its forces in obtaining Stepney-wide support. On Tuesday, 27 June, the police and bailiffs had entered Langdale Mansions, and a number of families had been evicted, but by Friday of the same week the landlords had caved in: £1,000 worth of reductions were obtained; £10,000 worth of arrears were ignored; £2,500 to be spent on repairs immediately, £1,500 each succeeding year. The twenty-one weeks' rent strike, bitter, bloody, had been won. Other landlords wishing to avoid trouble now became quite amenable. They, too, had learnt the lesson of Langdale Mansions.

These struggles became front-page news. In March a conference had been held in Stepney of representatives of London organisations and delegates from the Labour movement to decide on the co-ordination of the London tenants' struggles. Now the National Tenants' Federation began to organise a nation-wide convention. It was to be held in Birmingham in July, when representatives of every town and city in the country were to demand a new code for tenants and residents, a new Rent Act, and new standards of conditions to be provided by the landlords. A " Housing Charter " was drawn up, and a campaign begun. Labour leaders were drawn into the struggle. At the great demonstration held in Hyde Park late in July the speakers included Aneurin Bevan and Ellen Wilkinson of the Labour Party, and Elsie Borders, Michael Shapiro, and Tubby Rosen of the Communist Party. It was the latter who had done the work and the organisation, who had faced the bailiffs and the batons. Bevan and Wilkinson, as usual, were responding to the mood of the masses. The campaign was reaching its height, even during these menacing pre-war days and weeks, but then came the war and new problems had to be faced.

At the very commencement of the war the Government immediately introduced legislation to ensure rent control. Rents were frozen at the levels obtaining on 1 September 1939. The Government undoubtedly learned from the great Clydeside rent struggles in 1915, but a much nearer warning were the great rent struggles which were taking place during the months preceding the war.

Looking back, one can truly say that the tenants' and residents' struggles of those days were among the finest in our history. While they did not tear at the roots of capitalist economy, as did, for example, the General Strike, they immediately put the landlords into a panic, and began to focus the attention of millions of people for the first time on the housing scandal. The slum landlords and the building societies were very easily exposed, but, even more important, in the demands for lower rents hundreds of thousands of people learned to understand, through their own experience, the nature of capitalism itself. How could rents be reduced, argued the landlord, when everything costs so much? Look at the price of land in Stepney: £20,000, even £30,000 an acre. Look at the cost of building, and there you come up against further capitalist rackets, the cement ring, the steel ring, the timber ring. Would you like more facilities and amenities? Several landlords would say: " I would like to provide them, but all these modern labour-saving devices are very expensive. I cannot afford them." But then you discovered that they needn't have been so expensive; that the refrigerator which you could buy on " the never-never " for a total sum of £25 cost less than £5 to produce; that the electric cleaner which cost you £15 cost less than £2 to produce. And so in the course of those months hundreds of thousands of folk, who had mildly carried the burden placed on them, not only rebelled, but began to see who were the exploiters and their real enemies.

This growing political awareness was reflected in Labour's victory in the 1945 General Election. Many of the voters—stirred by the tenants' struggles, by the great epic of the Borders' fight against the building societies, and by the exposure of the National Government in its support of the building societies—turned with disgust away from Toryism to Labour.

One thing was in no doubt. Tens of thousands of working-class men and women had organised themselves for common struggle. There was a common bond between them, and in some areas, such as certain suburbs—where, as suburbanites know only too well, you could be living in a road for ten or fifteen years and not even speak to your next-door neighbour—this was indeed an achievement. All these people came together. Committees were formed and hundreds of people who had never been on a committee and had no experience of organisation or politics learned these things and learned them well. Outstanding were the women. Every feminist claim was proved. There was nothing that the men could do that could not be equalled by the women, and, in fact, they were mostly more enthusiastic, and hence more reliable. For example, during the rent strike at Brunswick Buildings it was the women who did most of the picketing. The strike lasted for eleven weeks during a severely cold winter, and braziers were lit in the streets to keep the women warm.

There was lots of fun, for Stepney people don't have to wait for a coronation or a jubilee in order to be merry. The jokes that were made about the landlords, the bailiffs, and the police were passed round from house to house and from street to street amidst great merriment. Some of them could not be put down on paper. Somewhere among my old papers I have a cartoon from, I believe, the London *Star*. Two working-class women meet in the street; one of them is wearing a very smart new coat. The other says to her: "That's a nice new coat you've got on, dearie—having a rent-strike down your street?"

The over-all solidarity was tremendous. Of course, there were differences, there were personalities, here and there there were "narks", people who wanted to be "in with the landlord" and would report to him what the tenants contemplated doing. But the main issues always overshadowed these things, and solidarity was the keynote. Tenants involved in a hard battle would be regarded as heroes, and their struggle followed daily by the whole of Stepney. You didn't ask what the latest cricket score was, but: "How are they doing over at Langdale?" In Langdale Street Mansions there are many Jewish and non-Jewish families living together. Many of the Jewish housewives would only buy kosher meat (meat slaughtered according to the Jewish religious law). Arrangements were made that the shopping for those on the picket line should be done by other women. Then this question arose of the buying of kosher meat, and conversely, of the orthodox Jewish women buying ordinary meat. (This may sound very petty, but to those who maintain this particular Jewish religious law it is a very serious matter.) Without any hesitation, and with lots of fun, Mrs. Smith would go to the Jewish butcher-shop to buy meat for Mrs. Cohen on the picket line, and the next day Mrs. Cohen (who would never have thought of doing it in all her life) would go to buy meat at the local general butchers for Mrs. Smith.

So far as the political side of the struggle was concerned, in the established working-class areas such as Stepney, Bethnal Green, etc., it was the Communist Party and its members which played the leading and outstanding role. Individual members of the Labour Party certainly played a part alongside the Communists, but never the Labour Party officially. In such cases as Feltham, for example, it was on the basis of these activities that the Labour Party won the support of the majority of the people in the Council elections. I have heard of no case where the Conservative Party or Liberal Party participated in any way whatsoever in these actions.

In Stepney the President of the Stepney Tenants' Defence League was Father John Groser, a very respected clergyman, whose qualities have won him a name far beyond East London. He was a Labour supporter, but without hesitation threw himself into this work, and when he—tall, white-haired, patriarchal in appearance, and in his clerical garb—together with Tubby Rosen, the Secretary of the League, stocky, aggressive, stubborn, went into action together, there were few landlords or their lackeys who could stand up to them. It was a great combination. One or two of the Labour councillors in Stepney and in Bethnal Green played a small part, but the outstanding role was played by the Communists, and this was widely recognised. At its height the Stepney Tenants' Defence League had three full-time officials—Tubby Rosen (Secretary) and two organisers, Harry Conn and Mrs. Ella Donovan. All three were Communists. The story of Mrs. Ella Donovan could be written separately, as an example to so many working-class women in or near the movement who never play their full part. They are shy, they lack confidence. Oh, no! they cannot be a secretary, they cannot write too well! Speak on a platform? Never! Ella was like this. But so rapidly did the campaign develop, so many things needed to be done, so many people were required, that Ella soon found herself doing many of the things she had hitherto thought beyond her powers. Then in a short while she was elected a full-time organiser.

As each day and week brought news of further battles in some new town or borough, one could almost anticipate the nation-wide rent strike which on one occasion Michael Shapiro forecast. Yet there were many places where no such actions were initiated. This was surprising, because public sympathy was widespread. Why, therefore, did not more people follow the example of the militant areas? In places like Stepney we could have done so much more to bring in the whole Labour movement behind the tenants' actions. The Stepney Trades Council gave full support, but the Labour Party and a number of the trade unions did not respond in any way. Were we too busy? However busy, we neglected a great opportunity of developing that unity in action, the lessons of which could never be eradicated.

It is not uncommon for Communists to become so submerged in

the work of tenants' associations that they lose their identity. This was not the case in Stepney. The Stepney Party in 1939, 500 strong, was carrying on activities, not only in direct support of the tenants but as an independent organisation in many other spheres, with a vigour equalling that of the tenants' fight itself.

I myself never held any position in the Stepney Tenants' Defence League. I was secretary of the Communist Party branch for most of that period. We saw our main job in relation to the tenants in assisting them in every way, particularly by winning wider support for their struggles, and explaining to the people the broader political implications of what they were doing. In the Tenants' League itself, of course, all kinds of views were expressed, and the Communists there made their contribution to the work, the same as any one else. That the Communist Party was recognised in leadership and responsibility was shown by the fact that I was from time to time called in independently, in order to help solve problems. On one occasion, in a very bitter struggle at Alexandra Mansions, Commercial Street, the landlord, having eventually agreed to negotiate, asked that I should be the impartial arbitrator between him and the tenants! It was a very strange scene that took place round the desk in this man's office, with Tubby Rosen and two of the Alexandra Mansions Tenants' Committee on one side, the landlord on the other, and myself as "impartial arbitrator". I think the tenants did fairly well out of that.

5

"Spirit Enough for Two"

STEPNEY IN the years before the war, and later too, was a political arena. Not only in the fight against the fascists and the landlords, but in the wider struggle for peace, in the exposure of the National Government, in the solidarity with the working class abroad, Stepney played its full part. In the factories, warehouses, and docks trade unionism was growing, and in all cases the Communists were playing a leading role.

The Transport Workers' Union (Docks and Motor Transport) was steadily recruiting, the Stevedores' Union was expanding, the Tailors' Union was being built up into a solid national organisation. Some years earlier some smaller Tailors' Unions had amalgamated, and in 1939 the Ladies' Tailors Union amalgamated with the N.U.T. & G.W. to form one solid union. Communists were elected to leading posts, and the membership has multiplied several times since those years. But the greatest drive relative to the problems was made among the shop assistants. The Houndsditch and Whitechapel Branch of the Shop Assistants' Union, formed in 1935, was built up at a rapid pace against many odds and difficulties. In Stepney and in the City of London nearby there are many warehouses where anything from ten to a thousand are employed. It was here that the organisation was taking place. Trade unionism gained better conditions for many of these workers. A classic struggle was that conducted in 1937 when the majority of the workers in a small warehouse employing not more than a dozen organised a strike, and stuck it for nine weeks. The strike was lost, but the spirit was not broken. The outstanding figure in all this work, though there were many fine workers, was Reuben Silk, still Chairman of the Houndsditch and Whitechapel Branch of (as it is now known) U.S.D.A.W. During the war, with many of these men being called up, and many going into more essential work, the organisation declined. But the Communist trade unionists who organised these workers in one of the most difficult industries were, in their own sphere, maintaining that same spirit which was then to be seen in Stepney in other spheres.

The Communist Party was campaigning on every issue. Individual Communists were working actively, and often in responsible positions, in all kinds of organisations. During these years international events began to take precedence. The greatest impact on the minds of Stepney people was caused by the events from 1936 onwards. Stepney is proud to record that the first three Britons to fight with the Spanish people against the fascists were Stepney boys who, in July 1936, were on holiday in Barcelona, and immediately the fascist revolt began offered their services to the hurriedly formed militia of the Republic. Nat Cohen, now an active member of the Sutton branch, was sent back home, having been wounded in the leg. Sam Masters came back for a short leave, returned to Spain, and was killed in action. Later many other Stepney lads volunteered and fought for Spain. Eight from Stepney were killed.

I would like here to speak on one thing at least that the Spanish war did for me. Whether justified or not, I am a fairly popular public speaker. I have prepared and written notes for classes for training public speakers. But when I joined the Communist Party in 1934 there were no such classes. You could either speak or you couldn't. I would have trembled if any one had asked me to speak on a platform. This is how I first spoke. On 8 September 1934 a Communist meeting was being held in Fulbourne Street, Whitechapel Road. It was a hot summer's day. There were to have been two speakers and several stewards and literature-sellers. Actually there was only one speaker, and myself as steward/literature-seller. The speaker was Lew Mitchell. He had the capacity for talking for hours on end, but on this hot day, after an hour and a half even he was tiring. The other speaker had not turned up, and Lew Mitchell beckoned to me and asked me to take over. I was scared stiff. I tried to argue that I had not prepared anything, I had not spoken before, I did not know how to speak, and so on. But I realised his plight and condition, and so I took over the platform. It may have been a brave gesture in so far as it relieved Mitchell, but it was catastrophic for me. The fairly big crowd that Mitchell, with his powerful voice, had gathered, began to disperse. I am not sure what I said, and later consoled myself that my voice was so weak that very few could have heard me anyway. After a quarter of an hour or so, Mitchell took over once again. When the meeting ended Mitchell said: "Phil, you will never be a speaker." I wasn't particularly keen to be a speaker, but this was a cruel blow. I asked him why. He made one or two remarks such as my voice not carrying. I asked him what to do. He did not know. In fact there are quite a number of such people, who are public speakers because they happen to have the knack, but they cannot impart their gift to others.

Because of this incident, though many opportunities were offered, I never spoke on a platform for nearly two years. During that time I held a number of posts in the Communist Party, and did all kinds of work, but I would not speak on a platform. The first week of the civil war in Spain I spoke on a platform. No one asked me—I wanted to. It was because of my earlier unhappy experience two years previously that once I began to speak, I took an interest in how to speak, and the problems of training others in speaking. These days hardly any one in the Communist Party would think of speaking without having had some advice and training; we have certainly progressed a long way since the time when I was a novice.

As a result of the many activities pursued by the Communist Party we grew in numbers, strength, and standing. Above all, perhaps, there was confidence. Confidence in the Party's policy, confidence in our ability to win the people.

The three-yearly elections for the Borough Council were to be held on 1 November 1937. These are held in the London area once in three years, with every seat being contested. In September, therefore, the Communist Party decided to contest two wards, Spitalfields East and Mile End West. We had contested these same two wards in 1934. The candidates were to be Lew Smith (now an active member in the Hackney Borough) in Spitalfields East and myself in Mile End West. I was then the secretary of the Party Branch, a post to which I had been elected in June. We were then participating in so many activities, and as secretary my mind was on so many things, that I was responsible for the mistake of attempting to take the election campaign in our stride. When the campaign was quite well advanced, and we made a check as to progress, I suddenly realised this mistake. The work had not been done, the organisation was poor, and the attitude to the election was almost lackadaisical. We pulled up with a jerk. We immediately made a review of the whole position, and whereas before we were contesting without any definite objective of victory, we now decided that we were going to win one seat. It was therefore decided not to contest Mile End West. A further decision was taken that I should be the candidate for Spitalfields East.

There was still a casual unscientific attitude to the election, and vigorous steps had to be taken in order to achieve the objectives set. As one example of this, we had an election agent, an active, earnest comrade, who was in charge of organisation and the election committee. When I attended one particular meeting I remember asking how many promises they were aiming to obtain. I was told 400. I immediately challenged this figure, and was told: "Well, we couldn't get more anyway." "But," I argued, "would that get us victory—and what was our objective?" There were three seats, three Labour candidates, three Conservatives, one Communist. The Communist Party was calling on the electorate to vote two Labour and one Communist. In 1934 the Labour votes had varied from 500 to 700, all three Labour being returned, with the Conservatives getting about 100. We reckoned that in view of the increased political activity and interest during the years 1933–37 there would be a higher poll. I therefore estimated that the Labour vote would now be somewhere between 600 and 800. It was therefore necessary, if we were going to win, for the Communist candidate to get at least 600 votes, so as to beat the bottom Labour candidate. To get 600 votes we ought to get about one and a half times that number of promises. Hence I insisted that we should aim at 900 promises. The election agent, and one or two others, thought I was crazy. The election agent had to be changed.

We got 865 promises. The actual vote was: top Labour 800 odd, second Labour 700 odd, myself 616, bottom Labour 570. The Conservatives once more got round about 100. This was the first Council seat to be won by a Communist in the London area. Some of the aspects of the election should be of interest because many factors play a part in political work, and there is no doubt that the people of Mile End returned me to Parliament in 1945 largely because of the example I had shown as a councillor when elected by the people of Spitalfields East. Those figures, therefore, make interesting reading. For this problem, as to whether Communists should stand for all seats in a ward or one seat out of several, tends to be a hardy perennial. The figures of the election in 1937 prove nothing except that each case must be judged entirely in relation to the local circumstances, and that no hard and fast rule on this question, which always crops up before elections, can be laid down.

Remember, we were advocating: vote two Labour and one Communist. We did not, of course, mention the names of the two Labour for whom the people should vote. On the other hand, the one who eventually did get the least votes was the most unpopular, and it was really him that we hoped to beat. The final voting figures were as follows:

360 Communist, first Labour, second Labour.
90 Communist, first Labour, third Labour.
80 Communist and two Conservatives.
80 Communist only.

There are many interesting deductions to be drawn. Firstly a point or two of explanation. Who were the eighty in the third category who voted two Conservative and myself, Communist? I should explain that Spitalfields is a part of Stepney where I lived a number of years, and where my father, a local tradesman, was still living and was highly respected. I, too, was quite respected and popular. As a matter of fact, one of the people who actually nominated the Conservative candidates told me he was only going to vote for two of them and also for me. He bet me a large Players that I would still lose, but hoped that I would get the Players. These eighty voters, therefore, were not political, but personal.

The eighty in the last category were obviously Communist Party supporters who were not voting as we had advocated, namely, two Labour and one Communist.

The fact must be faced that without either of these two categories expressing themselves in that way, namely, the personal vote and the " sectarian " block, we could not have won. Though my father, while a radical, was never a Communist, I think that the Party should be grateful to him and his standing amongst the tradesmen section for the votes they gave us that day.

There is a further important lesson to be drawn from the successive Communist votes in Spitalfields East. In 1931 the Communist candidate got 13 votes; in 1934 there were two candidates, the top one getting 98; in 1937 we got 616. There are many cases where the contesting of seats for council elections is not taken seriously. Recently, in several parts of the country, I asked the local comrades why they were not contesting the council elections which they had been doing for the past two years. All kinds of reasons, some very valid, were offered, but whatever the difficulties it is my firm opinion that the keynote should be consistency. It is important to treat the electors seriously. Most intelligent people know that you cannot win a seat immediately, and therefore you have to plug at it for year after year. They expect you to plug at it. Those Communist supporter votes are waiting to be cast. However inadequate the campaign, however meagre the forces, however inexpensive the material issued, only with the most serious deliberation ought we to refrain from contesting in a ward which we have been nursing and contesting in previous years. There are thousands of solid Labour Party workers up and down the country who can record progress in this way. This consistency has played no small part in building up a large Labour vote.

This election victory in Stepney was due to the all-round work of the Communist Party, but particularly to the political leadership which was already being acknowledged and of which this was a manifestation. The 1937 elections took place twelve months before the tenants' activities developed to the pitch of rent strikes, and the votes cast in 1937 were for the Communist Party's policy, its fight against fascism, its fight for the unemployed, and for the day-to-day issues which the Communist Party had been handling.

Some of my early experiences on the Stepney Borough Council are worth recording. The Council was composed of sixty councillors and ten aldermen. The political composition of these seventy was sixty-nine Labour, one Communist. The general attitude of the Labour councillors towards me was one of political hostility.

The most opportunist elements decided Labour policy. The vast majority had no Socialism, no aims, no fight. One of the questions which came up in the election campaign, as it does on every such occasion in every part of the country, was: " What can one Communist do on a Council?" If it was merely a question of numbers, and Right-wing-imposed decisions on the Labour Party majority, then the doubts of these people would indeed be justified. However, we showed in Stepney, as has been confirmed in other parts of the country where Communists are on the Council, that this question of influencing the majority is not a matter of arithmetic, but of politics. The main political arena was not the Council. The political issues were decided in the streets and in the homes, among the people. The Council was only the place where the will of the people was expressed. Without the mass activity by the Communist Party among the people, one, nay, even a dozen (as we have now in Stepney) Communist councillors must be ineffective in relation to the majority opposed to them. The reader can well appreciate that all the campaigns and struggles which are described in various parts of this record were brought into the Council Chamber. Very often my propositions were ignored, yet strangely enough, at the next Council meeting the same proposition would be brought in by the Labour Party. Why? Public pressure on the councillors, discussions at the Labour Party group meetings, reversal of previous attitude.

Some of the councillors seemed to think I was going to make revolutionary speeches, with plenty of blood and thunder. When, however, they discovered that my attitude was a constructive one, that the proposals I made were practical and based to a large extent, not only on Communist, but also on official Labour Party policy, the story went round amongst some of them that I wasn't really a Communist, but a Labour man in the ranks of the Communist Party!

At the very first Council meeting in November 1937 I was brought face to face with the bigoted attitude typical of the majority of Labour councillors in Stepney. I had heard that at the Labour Party group meeting before the Council meeting the group leader (Councillor Davis) had laid it down that in no circumstances was any motion of mine to be seconded by a Labour councillor. When Councillor Davis came into the Council Chamber that evening I approached him and told him that I had heard of this decision. Here I should point out that this was 1937, the year of the Coronation of King George VI. The Labour Party, the Labour Members of Parliament, and others had fallen over themselves earlier in the year in adulation of their Majesties. The then Mayor had received an additional £400 for expenses in connection with the Coronation.

So I said to Councillor Davis: "What will you do this evening if I move an emergency resolution extending the greetings of this Council to their Majesties? I hope you won't second me." Councillor Davis turned white, and stammered: "You—you won't do that, will you?" I said: "I am not going to answer bigotry with stupidity, but in future, don't be such a so-and-so fool."

I took advantage of that Labour group decision, for they cannot have it both ways. When an item came before the Council upon which I had strong opinions, and I would move its rejection or reference back, I was aware beforehand that I was not going to have a seconder. In the case of a Committee Report, the Chairman can only reply to such a contribution if there is a seconder. If there is no seconder, then the speech having been made, the motion for the reference back falls to the ground. Many a Chairman of Committee cursed the day that this decision had been agreed to by the Labour Party. For very often I would rise and make a vigorous attack on that particular item, exposing inefficiency, and, in certain cases, corruption; and while obviously some of my points could have been argued and disclaimed, the Chairman of Committee would be bound to his chair. He couldn't rise to answer because I had no seconder. The press naturally reported my statements. There was no comment from the Labour Party Chairman of the Committee and the readers drew their own conclusions. This, however, was fun, and the only fun, in this period of hard slogging and of honestly trying to win the Labour Party councillors to a progressive policy. I would like to, but I cannot record any big victories; so far as I am concerned, there were victories, but they came from the people, not from me or my speeches. When an issue which we were raising was near to the needs and desires of the people it was possible to get them to act, calling on their councillors, sending deputations, overflowing in the public galleries of the Council Chamber. It was then that some of the Labour councillors, succumbing to popular pressure, would modify their attitude. This position in Stepney doesn't necessarily apply to other localities, though my general experience leads me to the conclusion that very often, where there is 100 per cent Labour representation, complacency, and sometimes corruption, tends to develop unless the working class and their organisations remain vigilant and keep their representatives on their toes.

Those were busy times. For myself, I was secretary of the Communist Party branch at the same time that I was our only representative on the Council. Outside the Council and local affairs big issues were crowding the horizon. The Chamberlain Government was dragging the nation into war, supporting and building up Hitler to turn him against the Soviet Union in the East. On 11 and 12 March 1938 the Nazis, aided by their Fifth Column and the benevolent support of Chamberlain, marched into Austria. The Austrian working class, already persecuted and oppressed by their own fascist Government, were unable to make any effective resistance. The Communist Party was the only political party far-sighted enough to underline the danger of this action, and what it would ultimately mean to the people of Britain. As previously, when Madrid had been bombed by Nazi planes allied with Franco, we had declared in the slogan now famous and accepted: "Madrid today, London tomorrow." We now paraphrased this to: "Vienna today, London tomorrow."

A scene took place in Stepney on the night of 15 March which made me feel proud to be a Communist. An emergency meeting had been held by the Executive Committee and the London District Committee (of which I was a member) as to the line and action we should take. During the meeting I realised that whatever we decided would call for immediate action, and I telephoned the Stepney Communist Party office for a meeting to be called immediately in Stepney, to be assembled and ready when I came back to report the policy of the Party. This was about nine o'clock in the evening. Immediately the organisation went to work. The large hall (since bombed) at the Circle House was obtained, cyclists were contacted and were given lists of members to go and call out. The popular device of going into cinemas and calling on the people to come out was used again. On this particular occasion I well remember how Sid Carr went into the "People's Palace" Theatre, where a large audience was very attentively watching the performance of Unity Theatre's *Waiting for Lefty*. As many readers know, this famous American strike play is set in a Union Hall, and there are frequent interruptions from actors "planted" in the auditorium. When Sid Carr suddenly dashed in shouting: "All Communists and supporters must immediately go to Circle House", some of the audience must have thought it was part of the play! Anyhow, the theatre soon emptied, almost to a man.

The discussions at the special Executive meeting were prolonged and it was about midnight before it was ended. I managed to get a taxi, and reached Circle House at twenty past twelve. When I got near I heard the taxi-driver say: "Blimey! What's this?" Outside Circle House were hundreds of people. As I got out of the taxi, a cheer went up. I asked what was the matter, and was told that they couldn't get in. I still couldn't understand, and thought that perhaps the caretaker would not let them into the hall, but as I pushed my way through the crowds I realised that the hall was already so over-packed that this was an overflow which had been steadily waiting for three hours for the meeting to take place. I walked into the hall, and there on the platform were a number of the members of the Stepney branch committee, one of whom was speaking at the time. I gave a report of the decisions of the Executive Committee, and made proposals for the activities which should take place in the coming days. Questions were asked, and the meeting finished at 2 a.m. Immediately the meeting finished, Sid Carr, who had taken responsibility for this, organised some 500 of the people into scores of whitewashing and chalking squads. These people, most of them not members of the Communist Party, then spent the best part of the rest of the night chalking the streets of Stepney with the Communist Party slogans. When the Stepney folk woke up next day there was not a street which was not chalked or whitewashed. The following days and weeks were taken up with meetings, and all kinds of propaganda activity.

In May there was the first Czechoslovak crisis, when Hitler made his first move to annex Czechoslovakia. A big demonstration had been called in Trafalgar Square. A march followed this great demonstration. The march was to go by the German Embassy in

Carlton Terrace, to voice our protests, and on to the Czech Embassy near Hyde Park Corner to declare our support and solidarity. Several prominent people were appointed as a deputation, to lodge the resolution condemning the Nazi Government at the German Embassy; Professor Haldane was one of these. They went ahead of the main demonstration. The police, who were present in hundreds barring the way to the German Embassy, were aggressive and refused to allow them to go to the Embassy. When Professor Haldane insisted, he got a smack on the head from a baton. When this news went round the anger of the crowd rose. There were several demands to break through the police cordon, and to get to the German Embassy. The Stepney contingent did.

The police were drawn up in a double cordon across the road, standing parallel to the line of demonstration. To get into Carlton Terrace to the Embassy meant turning left into the police cordon. Contingent after contingent passed by, but the word had passed round and we in the Stepney contingent, by now veterans in street tactics, quickly took steps to break the cordon. The chief marshal of the Stepney contingent was Alf Kosky (now a prominent member of the Wembley branch), a lad with spirit enough for two people. I explained to him what we proposed to do, and told him immediately to bring forward as many men as possible to the front ranks, and particularly along the left flank; also to make sure of the quality of the two banner bearers. He himself took one pole of the banner, and tried to persuade the other banner bearer to give up his pole to another comrade. This lad, Jack Firestein by name, was only seventeen, and Kosky rightly felt that he should not have to bear the main blow of the break-through. But he refused, and insisted on holding the banner. (During the war Jack was awarded the Military Medal for courageous action at Anzio.)

The police were misled. The Stepney contingent marched right across the police cordon, almost the whole width of Carlton Terrace, and the police were under the impression that we were continuing in the main demonstration. When about fifty ranks had already passed, about 200 people, fronted by men who had been placed on the left side, were thus facing the police. I then gave the call " left turn," and the whole 200 marched straight into the police. Meanwhile, other marshals were bringing further ranks behind this advance guard. Within a few seconds, it was not four deep, but eight deep and fifty long, and within another few seconds it was twelve deep. This mass piled into the police. We broke through. There was a battle. This raged on the steps of the Embassy itself, and the officials looking out of the window could be in no doubt as to the mood of the British working class. Some people were hurt, and some were arrested.

I was in a bit of trouble, and I think I was saved by one of the outstanding accomplishments of Betty Field (now a member of the Hampstead Borough Committee of the Communist Party). This particularly remarkable accomplishment of hers was generally a source of complaint, but on this occasion I blessed her. I was battling with some police and one was about to strike me with a baton from the side, across the head. Betty had just come up at that point and was within a yard or so; as she saw this, she brought this accomplishment into play—the most piercing shriek east of Aldgate Pump! She suddenly let out such a yell that not only the police, but I myself, stood stock still. The policeman into whose ear she had shrieked dropped his baton and ran for his life. The others let go: Betty gripped me, cried "Run!" and we both ran. The Stepney Party branch banner had been torn to pieces, and the pole smashed. Some pieces had been saved, and with this aloft the contingent recovered itself and marched on.

This again was expressive of the militancy of the British workers and many progressive sections at that time. If harnessed and properly employed by the leaders of the Labour movement and their spokesmen in Parliament, the slogan of the Communist Party that "Chamberlain must go" would have been realised at that time, and Munich could have been prevented. Unfortunately, the leaders of the Labour Party, while expressing a few sophistries in the House of Commons, did nothing at all. The Communist Party was the only political Party, apart from sundry organisations like the Peace Council, which was actively conducting a campaign for peace and against fascist aggression.

In Parliament the only voice to be heard protesting against the betrayal was that of William Gallacher—but all the other Parties did their best to drown his voice when they cheered Chamberlain's announcement that he was off to see Hitler.

Anxious months passed in that summer of 1938. Then came the crisis. Trenches were being dug in the parks. The general fever of war preparation—" phoney " war preparation—was deliberately whipped up. Bluffing and counter-bluffing by the Government went on. After Munich it was Duff-Cooper, then First Lord of the Admiralty, who, when resigning from his Ministerial post, exposed the Government's " appeasement " policy, and the bluff which was being perpetrated on the British people. The mobilisation of the British Navy in order to impress the British public—not Hitler— that we were " standing firm ", the artificial creation of a " war " atmosphere by means of futile A.R.P. preparations, all this made it possible for Chamberlain to say he had " saved peace "—after betraying Czechoslovakia, and, in fact, making Hitler stronger than ever for the war which Chamberlain wanted to see between Germany and the Soviet Union.

At this time there was a ferment of activity throughout Stepney, conducted by the Communist Party. The Stepney Party decided to approach the Labour Parties in Stepney for joint action. I took part in the deputation which went to the three Divisional Labour Parties. First we went to Whitechapel and St. George's, where we discussed the matter with the then secretary, Mr. Morgan Phillips, now National Secretary of the Labour Party. In no circumstances would he consider united action with the Communist Party against the Government's policy. When he was then asked whether at least the Whitechapel and St. George's Labour Party would carry out independent action of its own, he replied that the Labour Party elected its representatives, and in this case their Members of Parliament would carry out the policy of the Labour Party. When asked where he stood on the Government's policy, he hedged.

When we saw the officials of the Mile End Labour Party, they were completely indifferent and defeatist. They were sceptical about any mass action, and tried to develop some anti-Communist arguments. That was how the Mile End officials of the Labour Party in 1938 were concerned with the questions of peace or war, of democracy or fascism.

Only in the Limehouse Divisional Labour Party did we get any consideration and a response. I was allowed to make a brief statement to the Limehouse Labour Party Executive; following this I retired. The E.C. discussed the matter and decided on joint action. In view of the rapidity with which events moved, such joint action never came to fruition, because within a few days the great Munich betrayal had taken place, and we were travelling downhill rapidly towards war.

But the Communist Party itself carried out many activities to indicate to the Government the feeling of the people of the borough. Such activities were being carried out in all parts of London and the country. Certain instances, however, were typical of Stepney. One of several I recall—I do so with a smile. One afternoon, at the time of the crisis in September, Pat Gold (now Mrs. Pat Smith of Hackney Communist Party) was talking to a number of women in a Mile End street about the crisis. They were immediately concerned to do something, and one of them said: " Let's go and see Chamberlain." There and then ten of them took a bus in Commercial Road to Whitehall to see Chamberlain. These were ordinary women, housewives; some a bit " rough and ready ", one or two very outspoken and capable of competing with any docker. One in particular was built on a " global " basis, and she had a way of sweeping aside everything in front of her. Arriving at No. 10 Downing Street, they were asked whether they had an appointment, and this lady answered, " Sure! " The doorman was a bit dubious, but before he could think he was swept aside. She entered, and the others followed. They asked to see the Prime Minister. Some junior official said this was impossible. They said they had time, they would wait for him. Meanwhile, the police had been called in, and a police inspector pointed out that they had no right to be there, and suggested that they should leave. " All right," said this lady, " shove me out." One look at her assured him that it would have taken a bull-dozer. A new tactic was then introduced. A servant came out and asked them would they have tea? They answered they " preferred peace ". The servant shrugged his shoulders—his responsibility was to provide " tea ", not " peace ". Eventually a senior secretary saw them, and from the description which I subsequently had from a number of the women who were there, that secretary had the most miserable half-hour in his life. He didn't seem to understand that he wasn't talking to diplomats. He was talking to Stepney housewives, who had the shocking habit of calling a spade a " shovel ". Never had such strong language been heard at No. 10, at least not from visitors. They let him know in no uncertain manner what they thought of Chamberlain and Hitler. At the same time they told him what they thought should be done, and should have been done, to maintain the peace of the world. Not the appeasement of Hitler, but the alliance with the Soviet Union and of all democratic countries was the answer. One and a half hours they spent at No. 10, and " never enjoyed themselves so much in their lives ". The enjoyment was due to a feeling of achievement.

When I heard the story later that day, I thought: " If that spirit could be multiplied only a thousand times out of London's millions, though Chamberlain could have his 400 majority, and though the Labour Party in Parliament was spineless, the Government would never have carried out its treacherous policy."

While the Communist Party was campaigning politically against the Government's policy, we had been demanding at the same time proper protection for the people in the event of war. The Communist Party had been fighting for some years before the war for deep bomb-proof shelters. In 1937 Professor Haldane, who had made a study of this problem in Spain, himself actively campaigned and wrote a book and many articles on the type of war we could expect, and the particular weapons against which the people need to be protected. The public, through official pronouncement and so-called " precautionary " measures, were led to believe that the danger was poison-gas. Haldane and others pointed out that the real danger would be high-explosive bombs.

The Government's betrayal of Czechoslovakia and its contribution to dragging the world into war was perhaps equalled by its indifference and cynical attitude towards the protection of the British civilians. We now know (though some of us knew at the time) that while the Government pooh-poohed the idea of deep bomb-proof shelters, in Whitehall and other places where very V.I.P.s sojourned, deep bomb-proof shelters were constructed fifty feet and deeper below the surface. In 1937 there were one and a half million unemployed. There was no shortage of labour and materials to prevent the building of such shelters, but the Government did nothing.

Unfortunately the Labour Party failed to campaign on this,

though Morrison, as leader of the London Labour Party and of the L.C.C., pressed the Government to make a greater contribution to Air Raid Precautions expenditure, which otherwise would fall on the local authorities. Neither Morrison nor the other leaders of the Labour Party were concerned about the quality of those A.R.P. measures.

The Communist Party was therefore the only political party campaigning on this question. In Stepney, a special committee of the Communist Party had been established, under the chairmanship of Harry Daile. This committee produced a document on how deep shelters could be built, reasonably and quickly, in Stepney. All kinds of technical points had been carefully considered, and there were a number of charts and sketches to illustrate these. This memorandum of some two dozen foolscap pages was ready by September 1938. We immediately decided that I should raise the matter at the next Council meeting, and meanwhile a copy was sent to every Councillor and Alderman, and the heads of departments of the Council. I asked at the Council meeting for a full debate to take place on this matter of such vital importance to the people of Stepney. The then Mayor, Councillor J. J. A. Long, refused to allow a debate on the matter. I was allowed five minutes in which to outline this document of twenty-four foolscap pages. When I finished my five minutes, no permission was granted for an extension. There was no seconder to my motion to debate the matter. We then went on to next business.

That was how Labour's representatives in 1938 showed their concern with the welfare of the people of Stepney. When at the end of the war another of Labour's Councillors, Mr. F. R. Lewey,* wrote a book on the blitz in Stepney during the period he was Mayor, it is strange that he did not show why the Stepney Borough Council took no action to provide deep shelters for the people. Mr. Lewey is a person of keen imagination. Those who study children know of the child who tells lies, not because of vicious or immoral motives, but because of the child's mind, which sometimes finds it difficult to differentiate between the real world and the imaginary world of its own making. Mr. Lewey has not yet grown up from that happy state of childhood. In his

---

* Mr. Lewey has died since this chapter was written.

book he says: " I had been agitating for a year [i.e., 1939] for more deep shelters." As Mayor of Stepney during the earlier blitz he may have *wished* that he had agitated for more deep shelters. But no one I have known ever met him in a state of agitation on this matter. Such people rely on the notoriously short memories of the public. (In Stepney they are less short than elsewhere.)

Frankly, I was very depressed. I had been on the Council some ten months and had met with much frustration, but I did think that on this matter, which they had been given ample time to consider and which was of such importance, there would have been fair debate and a decision taken according to the merits of the proposition.

But there was no time for depression. The Communist Party immediately had printed 5,000 copies of this memorandum, which were sold within a fortnight. Unfortunately, while the people of Stepney realised the value of our proposals, the general despondency which fell like a pall over the British public after those ugly September days also affected the people of Stepney.

Strange indeed it is to recall how at this period—1938 to 1939—the Communist Party, whose members played the outstanding role in the Tenants' Associations, was able to rouse hundreds of thousands, and indirectly millions, to struggle for improvements in their home conditions. Yet the Communist Party was not able to convince with equal effectiveness the very same people of the need for struggling for peace, and against the war which destroyed the very homes whose conditions were the centre of conflict between tenant and landlord.

The Communist Party did carry on throughout the whole country a powerful campaign exposing the Chamberlain Government. " Chamberlain must go! " resounded throughout every city and town, but Chamberlain did not go. During the spring and summer of 1939, after the Munich betrayal was confirmed by Hitler's annexation of the whole of Czechoslovakia, the demand was made for an Anglo-Soviet alliance to secure peace. But Chamberlain, while responding to the mood of the people, and sending office-boy emissaries to Moscow to create the impression that negotiations were proceeding, was, in fact, still strengthening Hitler. In the Labour Party election programme, *Let Us Face the Future,* published just before the General Election of 1945, they said: "Let it not be forgotten that in the years leading up to the war the Tories were so scared of Russia that they missed the chance to establish a partnership which might well have prevented the war." It is to be regretted that the Labour Party did not realise this with sufficient vigour before the war. Had they done so and, alongside the Communist Party and other organisations in the country, campaigned for this Anglo-Soviet Alliance, the war "might well have been prevented".

But now the war was coming and measures were being taken in Stepney, as elsewhere, to prepare for it. Not only was conscription introduced, but shelters were being erected in all parts of Stepney, and preparations were being made for the evacuation of children. The people would look at these shelters going up and would exchange remarks about their quality with the "brickies" and other workers employed on their construction. Almost every other street had its surface shelter, made of bricks, with a concrete roof. There were also underground shelters in the basements of houses, buildings, or factories. In no case were they deep enough to stand a hit by high-explosive. The surface shelters were meant to stand up to blast at a reasonable distance. No plans were made in the event of people having to stay in the shelters for any length of time. The idea seemed to be that the enemy bombers would drop some bombs and return to their bases. No one in authority foresaw the all-night and all-day air raids. Many Communists, including myself, joined as volunteer A.R.P. wardens. We carried out our duties, however galling. We distributed gas-masks to the people, while we wanted to shout to them "Demand deep shelters!" As Communist propagandists, we did that at the street corner, and in our literature and leaflets. As wardens, we carried out the duties for which we had volunteered.

On 1 September 1939 the German armies invaded Poland. At 11 a.m. on 3 September Chamberlain declared war on Germany.

6

Tea at the Savoy

WHEN THE war broke out the Communist Party was the only political organisation in Stepney to maintain its activity. Even the trade union branches had to protest against the directives sent to them by their Executive Committees that meetings should not be held. We were deeply concerned to ensure that the democratic organisations of the working class not only functioned, but functioned with additional vigour. The Communist Party set the example. The tenants' activities still continued. In fact, they were imbued with a greater militancy, and many hundreds of Stepney tenants not on strike, on the principle that we were all in the war now together, stopped paying rent completely. Thousands of pounds were never recovered by the landlords for the rents which were withheld during this period. There was a great intensification of A.R.P. propaganda, with the result that more surface shelters were built.

During the winter of 1939-40, at the period of the Soviet-Finnish war, the Communist Party in its propaganda sought not only to explain the war in Finland, but also to expose the Chamberlain Government's declaration that it was "fighting fascism". This we did by contrasting that assertion with the arms and support that were being given to Mannerheim, every ton of which was required for the defence of Britain. There was great confusion in the working class, and many of the Labour leaders deliberately created this confusion. There were some who tried to foment war against Russia, and to prepare the working-class outlook for that eventuality. In many parts of the country the Communist Party met with hostility because of this confusion and misunderstanding. The Communist Party of Stepney met with very little hostility, not necessarily because all the workers understood and supported our policy. Many did, as a result of years of continuous propaganda. Many others, however, who did not still had an abundance of goodwill towards the Communist Party. All the good work we had done in Stepney on behalf of, and in common with, the people could not be eradicated by the slanders and witch-hunts.

During this period many of our members were called to the Forces, including a number of our leading comrades. This did not affect the work. We took steps to maintain the organisation of the Communist Party, no matter how difficult. Directives from the London District Committee had urged that preference should be given to women to hold leading positions, and efforts be made for their rapid development. Some women thought that this was rather a belated measure. And in view of what did happen in Stepney, I am in agreement with that. Since then, however, I think that lessons have been learned. In Stepney a meeting was called of all women members, which the Branch Committee had asked me to address. This had never been done before. I was a bit nervous, but I didn't let them know it. The chairman was a woman, and I was the only man in the hall. It was an invaluable meeting. For them, I hope; for myself, I know. We placed confidence in the women and they took on responsibilities which they had never been offered, or volunteered for, before.

We seized the opportunity of the " phoney " period of the war, of the " black-out " and of the reluctance of many to leave their homes of an evening, to educate not only members of the Communist Party but others. We organised house discussion groups. Wherever we could get a room offered for this purpose, we would arrange for the calling together of a few neighbours in the street, or in a block of flats, and our leading members were specially allotted to lead discussions on topical and basic subjects in these homes. I remember attending such discussion groups. A dozen people, perhaps one or two Communists, and I would open on the situation and call for questions. This went on week after week throughout the winter months.

Then came the German attack on the Low Countries, and on France, followed by Dunkirk. A new Government had been formed. Chamberlain, though still with the support of half the Conservative

Members of Parliament, had to give up his post of Premiership. Churchill was now head of a Coalition Government—a Government which was meant to resist Hitler. This task, with Hitler now having over-run Western Europe, was more difficult than ever. We urged every possible effort to be made for the immediate negotiating of an Anglo-Soviet alliance. This was the core of all possible resistance to Nazi aggression. Chamberlain's plan of turning Hitler against the East had failed. As a Chinese spokesman said at the time, " The sky is black with the wings of chickens flying home to roost." Western Europe and Britain were now the victims. All the sacrifices of Czechoslovakia, Austria, Danzig, all the placating of Hitler with arms agreements to his advantage, all the economic assistance, all this gamble had now turned completely against Britain and the West. Was it possible now for a complete volte-face in British politics and for a solid line-up with the Soviet Union, which in turn would lead to the support of other countries based on this great bloc? That was what the Communist Party called for. But the Churchill Government did not respond to this clear and obvious line. Not till June 1941, after the blitz, after Yugoslavia and Greece had been occupied, after the Soviet Union was attacked, did this alliance come about. Meanwhile, the common people bore the brunt of the struggle and paid heavily for this policy.

But the people were beginning to resist. The apathy and indifference of the past months was now giving way to a new spirit of fight and hard work.

In Stepney, however, there was a new factor. The German Luftwaffe attacks on Britain, aimed at destroying the British air defences, had not succeeded, and the enemy turned his attacks on the civilians. East London was the first to get it. Stepney, lying alongside the river, Poplar and West Ham on the north side, Bermondsey, Deptford on the south side—these received the first blows. During the weeks of August the blows were relatively light. Small bombs had been dropped, of about 250 pounds, and not in very large numbers. On 7 September the main attack was launched. That Saturday afternoon we saw them coming over against the bright blue summer sky. We watched them in Commercial Road. A policeman said, " Better get in." We stood in a doorway and the bombs began to drop. They were bombing the docks, but some flights of planes flew across Stepney and straddled it. I had been having tea with Tubby Rosen in his flat in Commercial Road. Just opposite a bomb had dropped on a fruiterer's shop; we ran across and pulled the people out, and took a badly cut man to hospital. That night East London burned. The dockside was ablaze. This blaze continued for weeks, and was of great value to the German bombers, as it lit up a great part of East and South-East London.

When the "blitz" began there was renewed evacuation. At the beginning of the war children had been evacuated, and in some cases elderly folk. But the "phoney-war" period set in, and so the children came back to London. The London County Council was in a dilemma with regard to educating the children. Officially, all London schools had been closed, and the children should have been in different parts of the country to which they had been evacuated. In fact, thousands and thousands of London children were back in London, roaming the streets. Some elementary steps were taken to provide some education for them, and to keep them off the streets, where many were running wild. When the blitz came children and their parents, and many old folk and invalids, left Stepney. Not now in the organised way that had been carried out by the London County Council on Friday, 30 August 1939, but in haste and fear. They had seen death and destruction, and now the children wanted to get away.

Throughout the country billeting officers were hard put to find accommodation for all these Londoners. Many stories, enough to fill a book, could be told of working-class and kindly families who shared their homes and treated the children as their own. Unfortunately, other stories can also be told and, of course, as so often happened during those days, mainly we heard those other stories. Invariably where there was callousness, there was wealth. Many Stepney people, leaving Stepney that first September week-end in haste, went to country towns a relatively short journey from London. A number went to Windsor, where the only accommodation that the Conservative Windsor Council was prepared to provide was a cold hall, where they were told they could sleep on the floor. When they refused they were told by a Conservative Councillor that they could either clear out of the town or get into the fields.

Many of them slept out in the open, mothers and children, with nothing to lie on and no covering but their coats.

I remember how in Northampton a billeting officer went to the house of a friend of mine, who, with his family, occupied a six-roomed house. He immediately offered one room for evacuees and agreed to care for them. This billeting officer described how he had just come away from a house which had nineteen rooms, and was occupied by a young couple whose name is associated with that of a well-known make of shoe. The young lady was in the process of having a baby. She yet had several months to go, but she was able to show a certificate from the doctor, that because of the terrible trial that she was about to face she should not have any evacuees in the house, as they would make a noise. In the light of the medical certificate, the billeting officer was not empowered to take any action. Undoubtedly some mothers thought that children were better off not billeted in such places, but they also thought, " What kind of war is it? " and they must have had some bitter ideas on the Government's conception of " equality of sacrifice ".

The Stepney Communist Party was faced with these problems, and in many cases we would get in touch with the authorities, or with the local Communist Party, to help settle matters on behalf of evacuated children and parents. In these towns the Communist Parties did excellent work in this connection, and equally excellent work in exposing those elements who, while talking glibly of the war in the hotel bars, and while " playing their part " as officers in the Home Guard, refused to give shelter to the blitzed suffering children of East London, who had felt the terror of the bombing which these gentlemen and ladies made sure they never experienced.

The shelters, which until the blitz were deserted, were now packed to overflowing, and now the conditions were revealed. The trench shelters in the little Stepney parks were a foot deep in water. The benches were half-a-dozen inches above the water. It was quite impossible to use them, and certainly impossible to stay in them night after night. Now the street surface shelters were being put to the test. Many of them were destroyed.

The Communist Party immediately began to organise Shelter Committees in the shelters in order to secure proper conditions and to provide for the feeding and amenities in the shelters. This idea caught on, and within a short while was being carried on throughout Stepney and indeed the whole of London. Later the authorities took over certain responsibilities such as refreshments. The Communist Party was the first to organise entertainments in the shelters. The Unity Theatre did excellent work in this connection; mobile groups went to different shelters to sing songs and perform their lighter sketches. Later, other organisations began to arrange entertainment.

The conditions in the shelters were frightful. Most notorious was the Tilbury shelter, which accommodated several thousand people in conditions which I find it impossible to describe. Many people were without shelter, and every evening there was a trek from Stepney to Central and West London to take shelter in one of the basement shelters of the large buildings there. The next morning thousands of bleary-eyed East Londoners were to be seen on the buses and trains coming back to East London from the West End.

The contrast between the shelter conditions for the rich and the poor called for exposure. This was done. When the blitz had continued for some days, we in Stepney took the initiative. One Saturday evening we gathered some seventy people, among them a large sprinkling of children, and we took them to the Savoy Hotel. We had heard from building workers of the well-constructed and luxurious shelter which had been built for their guests. We decided that what was good enough for the Savoy Hotel parasites was reasonably good enough for Stepney workers and their families. We had an idea that the hotel management would not see eye to eye with this proposition, so we organised the " invasion " without their consent. In fact, there was some effort to stop us, but it was only a matter of seconds before we were downstairs, and the women and children came streaming in afterwards. While the management and their lackeys were filled with consternation, the visitors from East London looked round in amazement. " Shelters," they said, " why we'd love to *live* in such places!" Structurally, the lower ground floor had been strengthened with steel girders and by other means. But the appearance of the place! There were three sections. In each section there were cubicles. Each section was decorated in a different colour, pink, blue and green. All the bedding, all the linen, was, of course, the same uniform colour. Armchairs and deck chairs were strewn around. There were several " nurses "—you could easily recognise them. One happened to be standing around and she was wearing the usual nurse's white outfit, with a big red cross on her bosom. We were not quite sure what she was supposed to be nursing, but she was very attractive.

We had earlier appointed our marshals to take care of all our people. They immediately made contact with the waiters, and asked for water and other such provisions. The waiters were most helpful. We were expecting trouble; we knew that the management was not going to allow us to sit there, just so easily. After a few minutes the police came. A plain-clothes officer said to me, " What is it all about? " I explained. He said: " We will have to get you out." I said: " O.K.—I'm curious to see what you do with the women and children." (The blitz was on.) I said: " Some of these men have seen mass murder, God help you if you touch the women and children." He wasn't very happy. They tried intimidation, such as calling for identity cards, but we sat there.

The management was in a dilemma. They urged the police to throw us out. We were able to impress the management that any such attempt would meet with some opposition, and that some of his guests in the dining room were likely to be disturbed. The manager left. He agreed to ignore us; that was what we wanted. Then we settled down. The first thing the marshals did was to call for refreshments. Many of our people had sandwiches with them, and we therefore asked one of the waiters to provide tea and bread and butter. The waiter explained that they never served tea and bread and butter, and in any case the minimum price for anything was 2s. 6d. We said to the waiter: " We will pay you 2d. a cup of tea and 2d. a portion of bread and butter, the usual prices in a Lyons' restaurant." Three or four of the waiters went into a huddle, with one in particular doing the talking. He was evidently convincing the others. How they convinced the chef and management, I do not know, but within a few minutes, along came the trollies and the silver trays laden with pots of tea and bread and butter. The waiters were having the time of their lives. They were obviously neglecting their duties, standing around, chuckling and playing with the children.

The next day this news was flashed across the world. The contrast was made in bold headlines between the terrible conditions of the shelters in Stepney and the luxury conditions of the shelters of West London. As a result, the Home Office took special steps to improve the conditions in the Tilbury shelter and others. But this militant action led to further developments. A demand had been made for the Tubes to be made available as shelters. The Home Secretary, Mr. Herbert Morrison, said that this was impossible. The only valid reason he gave was that children might fall on to the line and be killed. This was not a very impressive argument, when you consider the hundreds who were being killed because they had no shelter. The police were given instructions to allow no one to use the Tubes for shelter. Loiterers were moved on by the police. The Communist Party decided that the Tubes should be open for shelter. This was done.

Two or three days after the Savoy Hotel incident preparations were made to break open the gates of the Tubes which the police were closing immediately the air-raid siren was sounded. At a number of stations these actions were taken. Various implements such as crowbars happened to be available, and while the police stood on duty guarding the gates, they were very quickly swept aside by the crowds, the crowbars brought into action, and the people went down. That night tens of thousands sprawled on the Tube platforms. The next day Mr. Herbert Morrison, solemn as an owl, rose to make his world-shattering announcement; the Government had reconsidered its opinion in the matter of the Tubes being used as shelters. From now onwards, they would be so employed. They were expected to accommodate 250,000. Arrangements would be made for refreshment and first-aid facilities. Later, bunks were being installed. "The Government had reconsidered the matter." They had, indeed! They had been forced to by the resolute action of the people of London which they had been powerless to prevent.

The effect of the blitz was disastrous—homes were smashed, factories destroyed, the docks put out of action, and Stepney denuded of population. Of the 200,000 pre-war population only 50,000 remained. The Communist Party was affected, but unlike other political parties, service to the people came first, and it rallied.

When the blitz proper began in September we had about 500 members. Within a week many of these were scattered, and of an evening went into the shelters. We could hardly contact more than two-score. An emergency Branch Committee meeting was called, and the whole organisation was revised. The principles were clear. The people were suffering, they needed help, they needed guidance. Every Communist must be organised to provide this. The slogan was introduced, " Stay in Stepney and stand by the people." Those who would not respond to this could not be considered for leadership in any capacity. A new Branch Committee was elected, composed of those who had shown themselves best able to carry out this task.

We had had eighteen street groups and nineteen factory groups. Some of the factories had been destroyed, but others had been evacuated. In other cases many of the workers had left. So far as the street groups were concerned, their activity was now redundant. In the evenings there was no one at home whom one could canvass or talk to. Therefore, while still maintaining the factory organisations, we organised shelter groups. A Party group in each sizeable shelter was what we aimed at, and in many cases achieved.

An important factor in rallying the Party was to show that the Party lived, and the action that we carried out in occupying the Savoy Hotel shelter did more to rally our members back once again into activity than a dozen circulars and notices. That action was received in Stepney by all people with great acclaim, and much fun. Communists were proud to belong to such a Party, and those who had relaxed and given way somewhat to the terror, once again became active. In view of the abandonment of the street groups, we set up a special street propaganda organisation to carry on the meetings, which in the normal way would have been the responsibility of the street groups. Those, too, after a while worked well.

Many of our members, of course, were now in the Services, and in various industries which took them to different parts of London and the country. I hope I will be forgiven my parochial pride if I say that most of these have carried the spirit of Stepney into the areas where they now live and work. I have heard of many cases. In some it hasn't been easy to convince other people of the correctness of certain methods or of the need for élan in political work. Often one has heard the remark: " This is not Stepney, remember," but in fact, while certain approaches might vary according to the political level, way of life, and background of the people, the *spirit* is a constant factor. Many a Party official in another London borough or town has had to acknowledge that what he thought could not be done, could indeed be done if the spirit was there. The excellent work of many former Stepney comrades in other places is certainly a great consolation for their loss to the work in Stepney.

During the war years the Stepney Communist Party campaigned for more production, for the opening of the " Second Front ", and for increased Army pay and allowances. Our Communist dockers, originally working in Stepney or other East London docks, were now scattered to all parts of the country. New ports were now taking the place of the London Docks, in view of their vulnerable position from the point of view of enemy bombing, and the heavy damage already inflicted on a great part of the Port of London. These men were setting an example wherever they were. Ted Dickens, Joe Cowley, and others are names which are now known in ports other than London. Some of the younger dockers like Bill Jackson were, of course, called up for Army service.

Stepney factories and workshops were now turning out only a fragment of their former production because of the blitz. Some of the secondary trades like clothing and furniture were producing less than capacity because of shortage of materials and labour.

Stepney during these years was a ghost of its former self. Those who knew Stepney, its virility, its movement, its bright shops, its cafés and restaurants open up to two, three, and even four in the morning, its informality, its thousands of evening strollers on the broad pavements of Whitechapel Road, would have felt the loneliness if they had stood in the main road about seven o'clock in the evening. Work had finished. People had gone home. Hardly any one was on the streets. Shells of buildings could be seen as far as the eye could travel along the road. And one wondered in those days what it would be like after the war; and then you wondered, when would the war end?

During the middle period of the war things began to move in Stepney. But then, just when we were waiting for D-Day, the " V.1 ", the " buzz-bombs ", began to descend and Stepney got its ample share. Later in the same year the enemy began to launch the " V.2 ", the rocket bombs, and a number did great damage in

Stepney. The very last rocket bomb to drop fell on Stepney, killing and wounding a large number of people. That was in March 1945. A few weeks later the war ended.

7

" As Ye Sow . . . "

NOW WAS to come the test. The war was ended; the General Election was to be held. The people throughout the country were faced with the main alternative of returning a Labour or Conservative majority. In Stepney there was a different alternative. A year earlier, when preparations for the General Election had begun, twenty-one Communist candidates were adopted in the country. It was decided to adopt one in Stepney, in the Mile End Division, and that I should be the candidate. How would the Mile End electors vote? Could we win?

The electorate had declined. There were only some 16,000, of whom 2,000 were in the Services. The electorate was therefore uncertain. The organisation was a shadow of what it was in the years before the war, in numbers, leadership, and day-to-day activity among the people. There were two other candidates in the field. The retiring Labour Member of Parliament, Mr. Frankel, and a Conservative, Squadron-Leader Motion.

We were confident we could win. The Communist policy was an important factor, but essentially, as understood by the electors, it was not so very different from that of the Labour Party. The factors which we felt would decide for victory were the support which was manifested for the Communist Party (and which had been developed by years of propaganda and explanation in countless meetings and countless thousands of distributed leaflets, pamphlets, and *Daily Workers*), and the memories of the great leadership of the Communist Party in the many struggles of the people, which I have recalled earlier in this book. There was also the good record of my own work in Stepney, both as a Communist councillor and as a Communist leader, which we believed was in contrast to that which the Labour candidate, and certainly the Conservative candidate, could proclaim.

The electoral machine began to tick over; the agent was Bill Carver, now one of our councillors. I myself was London organiser, and was concerned with the over-all problems in London, but I promised the secretary of the Stepney Communist Party, Mrs. Bertha Sokoloff, also a councillor now, that five weeks before polling day I would begin to work in Stepney full-time. Arrangements were accordingly made at the District Office. There was no question of making a mistake this time, as was made in the first election I contested in 1937.

Those who participated in the election campaign in Mile End, especially those who were working on the staff side, will agree that it was a great campaign, and one, irrespective of the result, which we all enjoyed. The main work was canvassing. There was all the propaganda usual at elections, printed material, meetings, loudspeaker-vans; but the really solid work which counted was the canvassing.

Early in the campaign we decided to test the feeling, and at the same time to try and get some indication of support, which in its turn would be heartening to our supporters, and also a strong incentive to the voters in general to vote for " the winning man ". Therefore, instead of collecting only the names of eight assenters, as is required by law, we decided to get 1,000. We got 1,700. This immediately raised the whole pitch of the election campaign, for it showed the strength of our support.

We made a calculation as to the number of votes we should need to win. A large number of people, though on the electors' list, had now left, and in turn, of course, other people were in Stepney who were not on the electors' list. It was not easy to ascertain this figure, and therefore we worked on the basis of the original list. On that basis we aimed at 6,000 votes, reckoning that of the 16,000, including 2,000 Service voters, 75 per cent would vote. That was 12,000. Anything round about 6,000, therefore, would give us a comfortable majority, for the remaining 6,000 would be divided between the other two candidates.

I myself took a close interest in the organisational side, but my main work was calling on selected people, taking up cases and problems which were brought to my attention, and speaking at meetings.

The taking up of the problems was a special feature, which was done in this manner. Our canvassers calling on people would come across some one who had some particular problem relating to the local authorities, the County Council, etc. At the end of the canvass such names would be passed through to me. I would then spend the earlier part of each evening calling on these people, and dealing with their problems. The latter part of the evening I would spend addressing meetings. Two hundred and eighty such cases were dealt with, most of them with satisfactory results.

We fought the campaign on the Communist Party policy, on the achievements of our Party in Stepney, and on my personal record. As against this, the other parties had nothing to offer. The Labour Party, of course, put forward their policy, but much support which this may have obtained was lost because of the ineffective record both of the local Labour Party, particularly on the Stepney Borough Council, and of their candidate. As the campaign developed, and the Labour Party began to realise this, they introduced slander and lies both about the Communist Party and myself. On the very last day of the election, posters were stuck up throughout the constituency, containing the vilest slanders against the Communist Party. I was very gratified to meet a prominent member of the Labour Party, who is still such, who told me that because he opposed these dirty tactics he was voting Communist. My experience has been, both in these and other elections in Stepney, that such slanders, which do " take a trick " in so many places, fail in Stepney, for they cannot outweigh the knowledge, experienced by so many thousands of people, of the good work of the Communist Party.

In the heart of Mile End is the London Hospital, the largest in Britain. Here there were 1,300 voters on the electoral list. Bill Carver approached the Governor, suggesting that an opportunity be provided for me to address as many of the staff who were voters as possible, adding that possibly an arrangement could be made for all three candidates to address them simultaneously. Captain Brierley said he would think it over.

Subsequently, he phoned to say that he was prepared to make these arrangements, and for the three candidates to speak in the lecture room, which meeting he would sponsor and invite all the staff able to do so to attend. Each one of the candidates would be given ten minutes (!) in which to state his policy, then a few minutes in which to answer questions. The arrangements, however, could not be carried out as Captain Brierley suggested, though, of course, we fell in with the suggestion wholeheartedly. Though the Conservative candidate was in complete agreement with the proposals, the Labour candidate refused to speak on the same platform as myself, though he had no objection to speaking on the same platform as the Conservative. Because of that, the arrangements were adjusted, so that each candidate spoke without the presence of the others. The Labour candidate spoke first, then myself, and later Squadron-Leader Motion. Before each went in to speak, we waited in an anteroom until the previous speaker had ended, and had left by another exit. (Incidentally, the Labour candidate, Mr. Frankel, refused to debate with me, though he was invited to do so by a trade union organisation.)

This meeting was perhaps the most exacting that I have ever addressed. I had asked my "campaign secretary", Maurice Essex, to come with me, and he later confirmed my own feeling about the atmosphere. London Hospital is one of the "classy" hospitals in London. You could sense the Conservatism as you entered the theatre. There was also a peculiar physical effect in that you did not stand looking at, or down at, the audience, as is usual when you stand on the platform of a hall, but there they were above you, in a semi-circle rising steeply upwards, you being on a level with the very lowest benches. You had the feeling that they were almost ready to fall on you, like a landslide.

The main problem, of course, was what to say. Before the meeting I had gone over my speech with Bill Carver and Maurice Essex—something which I cannot remember ever doing before. As I made my points I watched their faces, and I felt like a punter watching the field running with the horse he has backed lying right behind, yet nevertheless continuing to watch the race almost out of habit. I knew it was no good. None of us could think what I ought to say in ten mintes to an audience 99 per cent hostile, who knew very little about the real political issues, or about Communist policy. I tore up my notes, and I said that I would tell them why I am a

Communist. And as for our policy, I would tell them to read our literature. If they really wanted to know our policy, they would make sure to get our literature; if they did not want to know our policy, then there was no point in my telling them about it.

In the ten minutes at my disposal I told them how I was born a quarter of a mile from the Hospital: about my life and the life of others around me: the real cause of the poverty which they could see every day around them in the surrounding streets, how Communism is the answer to this state of affairs: what I, as a Communist, hoped to achieve. I told them the truth that I did not know how to explain my policy in ten minutes, and that if they wanted to know it, there was plenty of literature, and they should read carefully the election address and other material.

They seemed to like my honesty, and fired a number of questions, which I answered. Later on, from one or two friends at the Hospital, we discovered that Frankel had made no impression, that all that Motion had to do was to put on his best " Squadron-Leader " voice and say he stood for Churchill. That brought the house down, and no questions asked; but it was my brief statement which really got them talking. Whether we won any votes, I am doubtful, but I am quite certain that it did them some good, even if it was, for me, a most trying experience.

On polling day the Stepney Communists were everywhere. At one stage, at about four o'clock, it seemed that every one had been covered, and all our promises had gone to vote. At five o'clock a special meeting was called of leading officials in the election campaign, and new measures and a new spirit put into the campaign, to get every " possible " to the polling-booths. At last the day was over. A great meeting of Communist workers in the campaign was held. We were certain that we had won. Estimates of the results were announced, and proved, in fact, not very far different from the eventual count. There were three weeks between polling day and the count.

The count took place at the " People's Palace ", together, of course, with the counts of the other Stepney divisions, Limehouse and Whitechapel and St. George's. Mr. Attlee, of course, won Limehouse, and Mr. Walter Edwards won Whitechapel, both for Labour, and I won Mile End for the Communist Party. The voting in Mile

End was almost as estimated when we first began the campaign. The number of voters was actually smaller than we calculated; not 12,000, but 10,600, due, in a large measure, to a heavy number of removals and transfers. I received 5,075, Labour 3,861, Conservative 1,722, my majority being 1,214.

Certainly, so far as Stepney was concerned, the electors had shown that their memories were not short. The fruit of long years of hard work by many Communists had now ripened. The credit goes (as I declared at a " victory " luncheon) to all who had in any way played some part in the Communist Party. Even those who were no longer in it, for whatever reason, had, in their time, played a part.

I was reminded of this at the " victory " luncheon to which I have referred. This was held immediately after the result of the election was announced, and many of us walked in triumph from the " People's Palace " to the " Three Nuns " Hotel, Aldgate, stopping several times on the way to celebrate. Just before we reached the hotel, Lew Mitchell came across to congratulate me. He had left Stepney some years ago, and so far as I knew was no longer in the Party. We exchanged a few words, and I left him. When I was called on to speak after the luncheon, I recalled my meeting with him an hour earlier and I told all my comrades present, who were the leading workers in the election campaign, of my meeting. Most of them did not know him. I was trying to show the importance of every member of the Party. Lew Mitchell had indeed been active years earlier. He was one of those who helped me to come into the Communist Party. Later, for whatever reasons, he fell out, but he had played his part and all the hundreds who had been in the Party in Stepney had contributed to this great victory.

The General Election result was, as I heard it said, " the writing on the wall ". Soon we were preparing for the November Council elections. The whole Council of sixty was due to retire.

There are twenty wards in Stepney, each returning three councillors. Steps were taken to try and reach an agreement with the Labour Parties. We discussed the question at length, and for the sake of a united working-class list, we were prepared to compromise on a very low number of seats. The Party secretary was instructed to accept even as low as five seats. As we were overwhelmingly strong in at least three wards, where we could have captured all nine, the Labour Party knew quite well that this indeed was a concession towards unity, yet our offer was rejected.

The question then arose, how many wards could we win, and how many candidates to put up, and what should be the basis of our attitude to the Labour Party? We decided the last first. We still did not want to oppose Labour, we wanted unity, but the Labour Party had refused our offer. We therefore decided that no matter how strong we were in wards such as Spitalfields East and Mile End West, we would only put up two candidates, so as to leave one seat free for a Labour candidate. We did not need to discuss at very great length the question of how many wards we should contest. This was governed, not by our support, but by our own membership. During the war many of our members had been dispersed, the Party numbers had been reduced (there were then about 270) and we were all very much aware that far more important than the question of winning the seats was the character of the work to be done by our Communist councillors, if and when elected. We therefore confined ourselves to selecting a number of comrades who, we felt, could play a worthy role on the Council. We selected ten, and we therefore contested five wards.

In all but one there was a straight contest with Labour. In the other there were three Conservative candidates in addition. The Conservatives stood in about nine of the wards in all, but only in one of these were we contesting. This campaign was also organised very well on the basis of the experience gained in the General Election. There were some features of it which were, in fact, an advance. Outstanding was the number of comrades who in the General Election had played minor parts, and now held responsible positions in the election machine. In this election the issues were clear-cut.

The record of Labour on the Stepney Borough Council was, to say the least, a very dismal one. Corruption and inefficiency were their chief qualities. Against the policy of the Communist Party and their exposure of the Labour administration the Labour Party candidates had no defence. Once again they resorted to slanders, but without avail. All ten seats which the Communist Party was contesting were won, and in all cases very substantially. There was no doubt about the Communist support when Tubby Rosen polled over 1,000 votes against Labour's 500.

In March came the next test—the London County Council elections, in which we decided to contest the two seats in the Mile End Division, and the two in the Whitechapel and St. George's division. We were optimistic about the Mile End results, and we also hoped to win Whitechapel and St. George's. Our four candidates were men whose like the Labour Party could not show. Ted Bramley and Jack Gaster in Mile End, Michael Shapiro and Bill Carver in Whitechapel and St. George's. No Conservatives stood. It was a straight fight. Mile End was won.

This was an important result, for obviously many Conservatives voted Labour, and in my election eight months earlier the Conservative candidate took seventeen per cent of the votes. On this occasion, therefore, it was a clear majority over all who were voting against the Communist candidates.

We did not win Whitechapel and St. George's, but it was reckoned by some in the Labour Party that we had won it until the last day. It was then that the Catholic Church played a vigorous part in the campaign. Two features of their role, since repeated elsewhere, can be recalled. First the campaign of intimidation of all Catholic workers to vote Labour or else. . . . (I should here mention that one of the two candidates, Oldfield, is a leading lay Catholic, and the whole machine was brought into play behind him.) The other feature was a campaign of anti-Semitism. Michael Shapiro is a Jew. The appeal was made by the Catholic Church and its spokesmen to " vote against Jews ". Many of us were of the opinion that were it not for that reactionary Catholic campaign, unworthy of Labour or any progressive party, the Communist candidates would have won the seats. This opinion was shared by many Catholic workers who were genuinely ashamed of the anti-Semitic campaign.

Since those elections there have been further contests of the electorate in two by-elections which took place in December 1947 and February 1948. The first one as a result of a Labour councillor retiring in Spitalfields East, the ward which I have represented since 1937, was won by the Communist candidate with a much greater majority than I had two years earlier. The second was won by the Communist candidate in a ward where the Communist Party had only a very weak organisation, and where the Labour Party had put all its forces into the campaign. Both these elections were held at a

"AS YE SOW...."

time of intense anti-Communist vilification by every other Party in the country, by all the national press and the B.B.C. The Labour Party used every possible slander in both elections. These were not fought primarily on local issues, but on the more important national issues of the period. Once again I repeat that, while in face of the terrific anti-Communist offensive some Communist seats have been lost in other parts of the country, the only reason why the Communist party in Stepney still advances is because these slanders cannot obliterate our record of service to the people and therefore fall on deaf ears. In Stepney, at least, they "score no tricks".

Epilogue

This book, which tells the story of Stepney, may appear to end abruptly. But the story itself goes on.

A new phase has begun. Gone, for the mass of the people, are the days of enthusiasm and great anticipation. The future looked rosy to Labour folk in July 1945. But three years later the bewildered " man in the street " finds that his son or younger brother is retained in the Forces for a further three months; that the fighter-plane output is doubled; that obsolete naval vessels are being refitted. At the same time the violent anti-Soviet propaganda campaign and the attacks on Communism and the Communist Party leave one in no doubt as to the " enemy " against whom the fighter planes are to be used. War or bluff? Ask the wives of the men of the Guards Brigade, or the Hussar Regiment, who have been sent to Malaya to quell the fight of the Malayan people for their independence.

Scores of United States Superfortresses fly over our land. Thousands of United States Army men swagger in our country towns and villages, conscious of extra-territorial rights governing their stay in this country. An army of occupation. Whose war is it?

The people want peace, certainly the people of Stepney. They remember the last war only too well. Nor is it likely that the dockers of Poplar and East London, who destroyed Churchill's war plans in 1920 when they refused to load arms on the *Jolly George* for the war against the Soviet Union, will now turn against their comrades in that country.

Confusion and misunderstanding there are in plenty. Partly because of the intense and almost universal propaganda against the Soviet Union and the Communist Party; mainly because it is a Labour Government which is carrying out this policy of hostility to the Soviet Union. What the working class would never have tolerated from a Tory Government, many accept " loyally " from a Labour Government.

EPILOGUE

But the clouds of confusion thin, and even evaporate, as the very lives of the people are affected by the Government's policy. Take wage-freezing. The Board of Trade announced that the cost of living went up in one year by 10 per cent. The workers demand more wages to meet the increased cost of living. The trade-union leaders submit these demands. Simultaneously, many of them support the Government's wage-freezing policy. Hypocrisy? Humbug? Yes, and more. But this is the most symptomatic feature of this period. The Government's policy leads to the lowering of the workers' standards of life; while many workers may not be conscious of the errors of the Government's policy, they are conscious of its effect on them. Thought begins.

"But look at the laws passed by the Government to provide better health, housing, schooling, etc.," runs Labour's theme-song. Aye, and laws they remain, sterilised by Government restrictions and by the incapacity and passivity of the local authorities.

The Stepney Borough Council planned to build 1,300 houses and flats in two years after the war. One-tenth of this number have been built in three years. There is a waiting list of 4,000 priorities which never seems to get reduced. Twenty thousand houses are needed to modernise Stepney, and to provide all the amenities and domestic services that our people expect.

Health centres—the nucleus of modern medicine, the practical attempt to prevent, rather than cure, sickness. The heart of Bevan's National Health scheme. A good idea, a law. So what? The London County Council calculated that 160 health centres would be needed for the County of London to make the scheme effective. They decided to construct within five years—*one*.

New schools are needed to replace those which were "blitzed", and to improve on the barracks which went by the name of school when I was a child. Not one has been built in Stepney. The five-year-olds have nowhere to go, as the classrooms are already overcrowded. The teachers are working under strain. The existing schools are in need of paint, repair, and decoration. They are a disgrace. When you raise these things in Parliament you are told "we cannot afford it". But we could afford to spend £50,000 to recondition and decorate Clarence House (just one home) for Princess Elizabeth. No money? One hundred thousand homes could have been provided for "blitzed" English families for the money the Government spent on maintaining British troops in Palestine since the war. There is plenty of money around for the rich in profits and dividends, and for maintaining a capitalist, Tory, foreign policy, but not for working folk, either as wages or as decent social services.

The struggle for decent social services in Stepney is affected by national and international policies. Bevin whines that the Communists "stab him in the back". So whatever the Communists propose in Stepney is "only to annoy the Government". Thus harp Stepney's Labour spokesmen on the Borough Council. Recently they increased rents for new Stepney houses by as much as 2s. 5d. per week. The reason—that Cripps had raised interest charges on loans on housing from 2½ per cent to 3 per cent. The twelve Communist councillors opposed the increase. The Labour councillors resorted to the old theme that the Communists were making propaganda. It was necessary to quote an article by Dalton condemning this Cripps policy of increasing the rate of interest, to still the Labour councillors, but not to convince them. They voted *en bloc* for this capitalist policy.

So the hatred of right-wing Labour for the Communists ends with their defending the curtailment of social services for the people they presume to represent, and of imposing the burden of the Government's "City" finance policy on the homeless of Stepney.

The Communists in Stepney today carry on the fight of the old Socialist pioneers who worked tirelessly to rouse the East London workers against reaction, to organise them to improve their conditions at work and at home, to strive for peace, and in particular, for peace with our Socialist comrades of the Soviet Union. Communists today continue the fight that was conducted in the years before the war for the people's needs and interests. Now, however, we are pointed to as the main enemy. From capitalists and the Tory press we regard this as a compliment. But when it comes from right-wing Labour spokesmen—well, the workers must decide. Either Attlee, Morrison, and Bevin and their prototypes in Stepney are right, and the Communists *want* chaos and misery, or they are wrong, and in that case are taking their stand with the Tories as leaders of their type did in a previous decade. The people will judge.

EPILOGUE

In Stepney they will judge by deeds and by our respective records.

Do you remember how, when the new Parliament assembled in August 1945 the Labour and Communist M.P.s sang "The Red Flag"? No doubt Bevin and Cripps, when they now meet Marshall and Lewis Douglas, would like to forget that embarrassing incident. "The Red Flag" is not a song normally sung by the Wall Street millionaires. And for those who have abandoned the working class these lines are the most fitting comment:

> "It suits today the weak and base,
>   Whose minds are fixed on pelf and place,
> To cringe before the rich man's frown,
>   And haul the sacred emblem down."

Communists everywhere hold high the red standard of the working class. We do not wish to forget, we wish to retain that spirit. Our flag stays red.

NOTES

page 10, line 27
In *Left-Wing Communism – an Infantile Disorder* Lenin devotes Chapter IX to "'Left-Wing' Communism in Great Britain". The British Communist Party had not yet been formed, but its formation was under discussion by various groups. Lenin attacked the sectarianism within these groups, and wrote: "At present, British Communists very often find it hard even to approach the masses, and even to get a hearing from them."

page 33, line 25
The Housing and Rent Acts have been changed several times since this was written.